BY THE SAME AUTHOR

The Portable Virgin
The Wig My Father Wore
What Are You Like?
The Pleasure of Eliza Lynch

Making Babies

Stumbling into
Motherhood

Anne Enright

Jonathan Cape
London

Published by Jonathan Cape 2004

6 8 10 9 7

Copyright © Anne Enright 2004

Anne Enright has asserted her right under
the Copyright, Designs and Patents Act 1988 to be identified
as the author of this work

First published in Great Britain in 2004 by
Jonathan Cape
Random House, 20 Vauxhall Bridge Road,
London SW1V 2SA

Random House Australia (Pty) Limited
20 Alfred Street, Milsons Point, Sydney,
New South Wales 2061, Australia

Random House New Zealand Limited
18 Poland Road, Glenfield,
Auckland 10, New Zealand

Random House South Africa (Pty) Limited
Endulini, 5A Jubilee Road, Parktown 2193, South Africa

The Random House Group Limited Reg. No. 954009
www.randomhouse.co.uk

A CIP catalogue record for this book
is available from the British Library

ISBN 0-224-06293-X

Papers used by Random House are natural,
recyclable products made from wood grown in sustainable forests;
the manufacturing processes conform to the environmental
regulations of the country of origin

Typeset by Palimpsest Book Production Limited, Polmont, Stirlingshire
Printed and bound in Great Britain by
Mackays of Chatham plc, Chatham, Kent

Contents

Making Babies

Apologies All Round

Speech is a selfish act, and mothers should probably remain silent. When one of these essays, about pregnancy, appeared in the *Guardian* magazine there was a ferocious response on the letters page. Who does she think she is? and Why should we be obliged to read about her insides? and Shouldn't she be writing about the sorrow of miscarriage instead?

So I'd like to say sorry to everyone in advance. Sorry. Sorry. Sorry. Sorry.

I'd like apologise to all those people who find the whole idea of talking about things as opposed to just getting on with them mildly indecent, or provoking – I do know what they mean. Also to those who like to read about the dreadful things that happen to other people, when nothing particularly dreadful has happened to me, or my children, so far, touch wood, *Deo gratias*. Also to those readers who would prefer me not to think so much (because mothers just shouldn't), and to those thinkers who will realise that in the last few years I have not had time to research, or check a reference – the only books I have finished, since I had children, being the ones I wrote myself (not quite true, but it's a nice thing to say). And, of course, people who don't have children are just as good and fine and real as those who do, I would hate to imply other-wise. Also, sorry about my insides: I was reared with the idea that, for a woman, anatomy is destiny, so I have always paid close attention to what the body is and what it actually does. Call it a hobby.

'MARRIED WOMAN HAS CHILDREN IN THE SUBURBS' – it's not exactly a call to arms, and I do genuinely apologise for being so ordinary, in the worst sense. Here I am, all fortunate, living a 1950s ideal of baby powder and burps, except that, in the twenty-first century we know that talc is linked, bizarrely, to ovarian cancer, so there is no baby powder in this house, and we also know that the hand that rocks the cradle also pays for the cradle, or a fair amount of it, and that, for many people, babies are a luxury that they cannot yet afford. But even for the twenty-first century I am doing well: I have flexible work-ing hours, no commuting, I have a partner who took six weeks off for the birth of his first baby and three months for the second (unpaid, unpaid, unpaid). He also does the breakfasts. And the baths. So you might well say, 'Oh, it's all right for her,' as I do when I read women writing about the problems they have with their nannies or other domestic staff. More usually, though, when I read women writing about having children, it is not their circumstances that annoy me so much as their tone. I think, 'What a wretch, would someone please call the social services.' It is the way they are both smug and astonished. It is the way we think we have done something amazing, when we have done no more than most other people on the planet – except we, in our over-educated way, have to brag about it.

Most of these pieces were started after my first child, a daughter, was born. I played around with them in the two years before I became pregnant again, and they were finished soon after the birth of my son, so though the baby is a 'she', both children are in there, somewhere. The reason I kept writing about my babies, even when they were asleep in the room, was that I could not think about anything else. This might account for any wildness of tone. The pieces were typed fast. They were written to the sound of a baby's sleeping breath. Some were assembled, later, from notes, but I have tried to keep the flavour of the original scraps. This applies to all except the essay about UFOs (which was written before I ever got pregnant), and I do really apologise for writing about aliens and God and mortality when I should be talking dimple, gurgle, puke-down-the-back-of-my-Armani-jacket, but I wanted to say something about the anxiety of reproduction, the oddness of it, and how it feels like dying, pulled inside out.

Anyway, these are the material facts (for which I also apologise). I met my husband, Martin, a long time ago, we married I can't remember when, and after eighteen years of this and that we knuckled down to having children. It was not an impulse decision.

After our first child was born I worked while she slept, for the first year, and also in the evenings when her father came home. When she was one, she went to a nursery for (count them) six and a half hours per day, three of which were spent having a nap. When she was two and a half, she got a baby brother, and I worked while he slept. And so on. I would really like a rest, now.

Finally, and quietly, I have to apologise to my family and hope that they will forgive me for loving them in this formal, public, plundering way. Starting with my own mother – whose voice comes through my own, from time to time – and working down the generations. Like all women who write about their children, I have a wonderful partner – except in my case it is true. I also have to apologise to my children for writing about their baby selves; either too much, or not enough, or whatever changing way this book takes them, over the years.

My only excuse is that I think it is important. I wanted to say what it was like.

Anne Enright
September 2003

Breeding

Growing up in Ireland, we didn't need aliens – we already had a race of higher beings to gaze deep into our eyes and force us to have babies against our will: we called them priests. It is great being Catholic. A loopy Protestant, on the other hand, has to make it up as she goes along. And no one makes it up better than your American Protestant, driven mad by all that sky. In the 1980s, while we were fighting for contraception and abortion, they were fighting for the future of the human race. I am talking about those people who are forced to carry alien foetuses against their knowledge or will. In 1994 it was said that the alien breeding programme had already affected 'up to two million' carefully selected Americans. What I want to know is – who was counting? How do you get on this programme? And why do you have to be white to qualify?

Not that I am smug about being Irish, Catholic and obliged to give birth in a field – personally I would rather see a flying saucer than a vision of the Virgin Mary, I think it would be less frightening. The alien breeding programme that leaves strange bruises around the genitals of middle America, though spooky, may just have been preferable to the vicious fight in Ireland over who owns your insides. 'Get your rosaries off our ovaries,' was the battle cry as we voted, over and over, for or against abortion, while the pro-life louts hung around the Dublin streets with their short hair and jars full of dead baby. I used to live in the centre of town and passed them on my way to the shops, waving their grim placards. Instead of spitting or shouting, I would amuse myself by imagining shafts of light with small putty-coloured creatures floating in them; creatures with rubbery fingers and blank, shiny eyes. Because nothing looks more like a foetus, of course, than your average small grey from beyond the Horsehead Nebula.

Never mind the folk legends, the *National Enquirer,* or trash paranoia on the Internet, for easy reference aliens in America can be sorted into two types – boys' aliens and girls' aliens. The boys' aliens are the ones that everyone knows about. They fly around the place in different-shaped craft, many of which could turn on a dime. They come from big mother ships that are so big you just couldn't say how big they are. These craft appear over long roads and in big skies; they glow strangely and don't do a lot – a few scorch marks in the grass, a crop circle, some mutilated cattle. The CIA know all about boys' aliens, the radar blips and the pilot's black box, because boys can not only verify their aliens scientifically, they also suspect other boys of conspiring to cover this proof up.

Girls do not deal in proof. Girls' aliens happen under the skin. Girls' aliens make you fall in love; they manifest themselves in the things that you have forgotten, until you remember it, all in a rush. Despite the fact that girls not only meet the aliens, but also have their babies, they do not remember their impregnation, except under hypnotic regression. How can Hollywood get it so wrong? There are no tentacles, and no one speaks English – aliens have no need of mere speech. There are enough transcripts of these women weeping as they recover the details of their alien abduction for us to arrive at a reasonably consistent anatomy. We're talking three fingers here, not five, or none, or six. Aliens have no knuckles, no knees, and no muscular structure. They have difficulty walking. Their mouths never open when they speak. Above all, aliens never ever have sexual organs and a pregnant alien is a contradiction in terms.

Things move fast in the alien business. Abductees are so up in the nature of the beasts that float them out of their cars or beds on shafts of light that, though distressed, they are never old-fashioned. 'There was just this usual grey crap,' says one woman, recovering her first memory of being on board an alien craft. Still, they are surprisingly hard to describe. At the borders of conscious memory, when they are walking around our planet, aliens may use strange props, something slightly 'off': a stetson hat of unnatural size, a miner's lamp, or a false moustache pinned beneath a non-existent grey nose. The silver suits of the fifties are well gone, as are the space-bitches of the sixties: 'I am Lamxhia and I need your earth sperm.' When you're on the ship these days, with your clothes in a heap on the floor, lying on a one-legged table with your ankles in (optional) stirrups, there are only two types of alien – small greys and tall greys. Small greys move you around despite your protests and the fact that your legs don't work, and when they have attended to all those little surgical details, taking tissue, scraping out eggs, putting in foetuses or nasal implants or the small implant that goes in the back of your calf, then it's time for the tall grey to come in, wave them off, and gaze deep into your eyes. This is the moment when it all makes sense. Aliens' eyes are large, lanceolate and black, they are non-reflective and

7

have no pupils. It is a terrifying thing to look into an alien's eyes, but, against your will, you may find yourself saturated with emotion and a sense of meaning; helpless with love.

Abductees are 94 per cent Caucasian, 75 per cent female and they have 1.9 children. All of them arrive at the hypnotherapist's office seeking help, frightened and distressed, with a story about missing time. They saw something strange at the foot of the bed, they saw something strange at the side of the road – then it's two hours later and they are in the wrong place with no idea how they got there. They are heading south on the wrong highway and the tank is still full of gas. They wake with the sheets awry and a husband who is sleeping too soundly. They arrive for work two hours late with their blouse on the wrong way around. (You see? It's happened to you.)

What they remember, eventually, is a hidden reproductive history. Men may have their sperm mechanically harvested, in a sudden access of unwelcome pleasure, but it is the women (mostly) who get pregnant. The pregnancy will subsequently disappear, with no evidence of a miscarriage. Sometimes the hymen is left unbroken. Where does the foetus go? On the spaceship, victims might see rows of jars with something growing in them; whole walls or rooms full of them. They might remember, like Debbie Tomey, being spreadeagled on a table with 'a terrible pressure within her loins', shouting, 'It's not fair! It's mine! It's mine!' They might remember later – years later – meeting a slender, hybrid daughter with ivory skin, no eyebrows, and sparse, cotton-coloured hair.

One of the main practitioners in the field of hypnotic regression is Budd Hopkins, the New York artist who stumbled into the aliens business when an article he wrote for the *Village Voice*, SANE CITIZEN SEES UFO IN NEW JERSEY, won him a postbag of frightened people who wanted to know what had happened to them after they, too, saw a strange light in the sky. He is now experienced in the techniques of hypnotic regression, or assisted imagination – 'Let's *allow* it to start getting dark in the room . . . I want you to *get the feeling* of getting into your bed.' His abductees have group therapy sessions to deal with their sense of isolation, helplessness and overwhelming anger. They are now abducted so regularly, they don't know what to do any more. Their children are abducted, their parents are abducted, and their grandparents feel a bit off-colour.

Budd seems like a nice man – like many other regression therapists who investigate alien abduction. Many are handsome in a rugged kind of way and admit to being brought up as 'strict materialists'. They really do want to do something. They really don't know what is going on. Their world view has been exploded by a series of highly distressed women whom only they can help. The women's sincerity, the weirdness of their accounts, the fact that they are so normal (read stupid), convinces them that 'she couldn't be making it all up'. How, for example, could you make up the detail about a small grey trying on your shoes? Speaking as someone who makes things up for a living, who can spot a 'strict materialist' from five hundred paces, I think the shoes are a nice detail, as is the green elevator shaft with eyes, and the man in blue striped pyjamas.

Nine of Hopkins's abductees were tested blind by an independent psychologist who found them to be 'of above average intelligence', with a 'considerable richness of inner life', which is tied to a 'risk of being overwhelmed by the urgency of their impulses'. They suffer from lowered self-esteem and relative egocentricity. Under stressful conditions 'at least six of the nine showed a potential for more or less transient pyschotic experiences . . . with confused and disordered thinking that can be bizarre, peculiar, or very primitive and emotionally charged'. These people are not pathological liars, paranoid schizophrenics or hysteroid characters subject to fugue states and/or multiple personalities. They are normal. They are not making it up – at least, they don't know that they are making it up. Perhaps you could say that the story is making them up instead.

Time was, people who suffered childhood sexual abuse were accused of 'making it all up'. As many as 35 per cent of abductees were also abused, yet they are 'making up' something else entirely. As therapist John Mack (Ph.D.) points out, regression therapy moves through dissociative strategies and false memories to approach the real facts of a patient's past. The difference with his patients is that some of them have a *false* memory of sexual abuse, which in fact covers the real story of alien abduction. It is only of limited use asking whether this man should be in jail.

Whatever the facts, there is a considerable amount at stake here: the word 'hysteric' is as charged and as complicated as the women it tries to identify. Besides, what about all those, to quote one abductee, 'Baby things. Baby here. Baby there. Baby everything. Everything is babies. Oh, God, I mean like babies, OK?'

The first foetus to star in a movie was the one in *2001: A Space Odyssey*, a star child, the first of a new hybrid race. I wonder if the actor was ever born.

The first female protagonist of a Hollywood science fiction film was Sigourney Weaver in *Alien* – a film so saturated with reproductive anxiety it still makes you check for something stirring in your guts. (Is that a tapeworm, or was it just wind?)

Look at a copy of the *National Geographic*, a magazine that will always exist in 1973, and there it is – between a photo essay on the birth of a distant galaxy and an article about breast decoration among the Nuba, floats the foetus, 'the world within'. It drifts free, like an astronaut on his umbilical cable; glowing, weightless; with pads for fingers, and plum-like, radioactive eyes. The foetus sees nothing, knows everything. It does not eat, or speak – the mouth is a bare line – but it seems to smile. It lives in water. It is a different life form. The foetus has no capacity for wonder. There is something blank and mean-spirited about it, perhaps. It lurks. It is all potential. We do not know if it means us well.

As Julia Kristeva says, quoting Mallarmé, '"What is there to say concerning childbirth?" I find that question much more pungent than Freud's well-known "What does a woman want?" Indeed, what does it mean to give birth to a child? Psychoanalysts do not talk much about it.'

What is it like being pregnant? 'It is like having an alien inside you,' a woman said to me, many years ago. 'No really, it is.' She had three.

We do not choose, sometimes, to be occupied by this other creature, and this is one reason why women find pregnancy unsettling. It is assumed that our bodies will 'know', even if we don't, what pregnancy is like and what it is for; that we are, on some cellular level, wise, or even keen on the reproductive game. But I do not know how such cellular knowledge might happen, or where it might inhere.

A woman probably does know what she wants when she says, 'I want a baby,' because a baby is, first and foremost, an act of the imagination (unless it is an act of fourteen tequilas after the office do). But there are many cases of women who do not know that they are pregnant until they go into labour. There are cases of woman who 'know' that they are pregnant, but who are not. In discussions about reproductive choice, it seems to me that we do not know what we are talking about, or that different people are talking about different things, and the experience of pregnancy, because it is so difficult to describe, is skipped or ignored.

In Ireland the imagination is still held in high regard. 'Making things up' is a normal and often social activity. This has its drawbacks, of course. There are always the priests, some of them abusive – and the babies. In Ireland we have babies all the time. Easy-peasy. We have them just like that.

'I think you should forget about aliens,' says Gerry, my friend. 'All that nonsense. Have a baby instead.'

And I say, 'Watch the skies.'

The Glass Wall

I spent most of my thirties facing a glass wall. On the other side of this wall were women with babies – 'mothers', you might call them. On my side were women who simply *were*. It didn't seem possible that I would ever move through the glass – I couldn't even imagine what it was like in there. All I could see were scattered reflections of myself; while on the other side real women moved with great slowness, like distantly sighted whales.

I always assumed I would have children, but only dimly – I never thought about when. I was reared in the seventies, by a woman who had been reared in the thirties, and we were both agreed that getting pregnant was the worst thing that could happen to a girl. My mother thought it would ruin my marriage prospects and I thought it would ruin my career prospects (same thing, really, by the different lights of our times). And when do you stop being a girl? By 'career' I meant something more than salary. I could not get pregnant, I thought, until I had 'gotten somewhere', until I 'knew who I was', until I was, in some way, more thoroughly myself.

These things are important: they do happen, but they often happen late, and you can hardly tell people to stop dithering.

I look at women in their thirties with their noses pressed up against the glass, and all I can tell them (wave!) is that life in here on the other side is just the same – only much better, and more difficult.

I see them wondering, Does he love me and do I love him? and Will I have to give up smoking? and What about my job? and I don't want to be that fat woman in the supermarket, and What if it is autistic and Don't they cry all the time? and I want to say, 'It's fine.' More than that, when I first had a child, I was so delighted, I wanted to say, 'Do whatever it takes.' Children seemed to be such an absolute good, independent of the relationship that made them, that I wanted to say, 'Buy one if you have to,' or, 'Hurry.'

I was wrong, of course. Besides, most women are more interested in sexual love than they are in the maternal variety, they want a man more than they want children, or at least they want it *first*. Still, it is good to keep in mind the fact that, in a world where sexual partners can come and go, children remain. They are our enduring love.

Dream-Time

One Friday in October I started falling in love with everyone, and I stayed in love for two weeks, with everyone. This was awkward. It was a moony, teenage sort of love. I waited for the phone to ring. I was shy, almost anguished. I missed appointments, even with the people I loved, which was everyone, and so stayed at home and saw no one, my mind full of impossible thoughts.

I did manage to go to a school reunion (where I loved them all) and to the opening night of a play (where I made some wonderful new friends), but mostly I mooched, and wrote letters to celebrate the fact that I had just finished a book and that life was, perhaps unbearably, good.

Towards the end of this peculiar fortnight, I had a dream full of the usual suspects: people from my past who spoke to me in an unsettling, unresolved way. I have this dream, with variations, all the time, but this night it was interrupted by a woman I barely knew twenty years ago who floated in through a window, dressed in pink. She smiled an angelic smile, as if to say, 'None of this matters any more,' and then she patted her stomach, very gently. I started awake with the thought that I was pregnant; then I turned over to go back to sleep, saying to myself that the moment had come: it was time to stop the shilly-shally, the hit-and-miss, we had to get this conception thing going, properly, finally, and have the baby that was waiting for us, after all these years.

Soon after, I went to Berlin for a reading, half-dreading who I might be obliged to fall in love with there – but sometime in the middle of the weekend, I hit a wall. I couldn't say why this was. I didn't tell my hosts that I knew German and disliked the half-understood conversations they held in front of me, before turning to talk English with a smile. I walked the streets, planning a story about a woman who falls in love all the time, and another story that was full of mistranslation and sly insinuation, in which a woman meets a foreign couple and cannot quite tell what is going on.

My hostess said that she loved the passage in my book about a dream in which the ceiling is full of dangling penises. I have never written such a passage, nor anything like it, but she insisted: she was even quite insulted, as though I were accusing *her* of having my own pornographic thoughts. What could I say? I said I would check. But I noticed, in myself, a terrible physical weight, as if I could not carry my life around any more, I could not even lift it off the chair. I thought that perhaps I should stop writing books: something, at any rate, had to change. I walked from Schönhauser Allee to Unter den Linden, looking at the afternoon moon over Berlin, thinking that when it was full my period would come and then maybe everything would right itself again.

On the way back, I stopped over in London and got very drunk. The hangover seemed to last a week. I felt terrible. I dosed myself with miso soup and seaweed. I was insane for miso soup and seaweed. I still thought my life must change. I went on the Internet and typed in 'ovulation' on the search engine, then turned to my husband, Martin, saying, 'I think this beer is off. Is there something wrong with this beer?'

We bought the pregnancy test from a girl with romantic thoughts behind the cash register in Boots. Martin says I was delighted when it proved positive, but I was not delighted, I was shocked and delighted maybe, but I was mostly deeply shocked.

If Kafka had been a woman, then Gregor Samsa would not have turned into an insect, he would not have had to. Gregor would be Gretel and she would wake up one morning pregnant. She would try to roll over and discover she was stuck on her back. She would wave her little hands uselessly in the air.

It seems to me that I spent the next six weeks on the sofa listening to repeats of radio dramas, but my computer files record the fact that I worked, and that I also surfed the Net. I was looking for information on what happens when you get drunk in the very early stages of pregnancy, but the women on the Internet all wanted to lock expectant mothers up for drinking Diet Coke. In the chat rooms and on the notice-boards all the pregnant women talked about their pets: the cat who just knew, the dog who got upset. There was also a lot of stuff about miscarriages.

Martin took me up the mountains to keep me fit and I nearly puked into the bog. I got stuck on one tussock and could not jump to the next. The life inside me was too delicate, and impossible and small. No jumping, no running, no sex, no driving, no drink, no laughs, no household cleaning, no possibility, however vague or unwanted, of amorous adventures, no trips to India, no cheerful leaps from one tussock to the next in the god-damn bog. I made the jump anyway and went over on my ankle. Darkness started to fall.

The next weekend he brought me to Prague, as a surprise. There are two things in my life that I have never turned down, one is a drink and the other is an aeroplane ticket. Already, friends were starting to look askance when I stuck to water; now I sat in the departures lounge and did not want to board the plane. This intense reluctance, this exhaustion, was pregnancy. It was nine in the morning. People were running to the gates, buying newspapers, checking their boarding passes and drinking prophylactic shots of whiskey. I looked at the world around me and listened to my own blood. There was a deep note humming through me, so low that no one else could hear. It was in every part of me, swelling in my face and hands, and it felt like joy.

The weeks when you are generally, as opposed to locally, pregnant are a mess. I put on weight in odd places. I went to the kitchen in the middle of the night to see what nameless but really specific thing I was starving for. I sat down on the floor in front of the open fridge and cried. The aisles of the supermarket were filled with other possibly pregnant women – paralysed in front of the breakfast cereals, stroking packets of organic lentils, picking up, and setting down again, a six-pack of Petits Filous. Starvation is no joke, especially when you have been eating all day. I had, in my life, managed to have every neurosis except the one about food, and now my body was having it for me.

At ten weeks I went to the obstetrician, as if she could somehow fix what was wrong with me. We talked about postnatal depression (could I be having it already?). We talked about amniocentesis, but not much. She did not seem to realise that the child I had inside me would have to be deformed. She led me up a terrazzo staircase that smelt of school, and brought me into a dark room. 'Right,' she said, flicking on the light. 'Let's have a look.' I was expecting stirrups, but instead I got an ultrasound. The baby was like a little bean sprout. It flicked and jumped, as though annoyed to be disturbed. She lingered, with her sonic pen, as though this sight amazed her every time. It was all too much to bear. I said, 'It looks a bit disgusting,' and she said, 'Don't be silly,' as though she knew I was just shamming.

All of a sudden I was going to have a baby. The fact of my pregnancy was as real and constant to me as a concrete block in the middle of the room, but I still did not know what it meant. A baby. A baby! I had to realise this many times: first with a premonition, then with a shock. I had to realise it slowly, and I had to realise the joy. After the ultrasound, it came to me all in a clatter and I walked home, roaring it out in my head. That night we went out to tell my parents. My mother said very little but, every time I looked at her, she looked five years younger, and then five years younger again. She was fundamentally, *metabolically* pleased. She was pleased all the way through, as I was pregnant all the way through.

I spent the next six months remembering and forgetting again, catching up with what my body already knew. The world senses this gap. It seemed like everyone was trying to persuade me into this baby, as though they had made a great investment in me, and didn't trust me to take care of it. Out of badness, I did my best to drink (and failed) and took an occasional cigarette. This made one woman, a practical stranger, burst into tears. I wondered what her mother was like.

A pregnant woman is public property. I began to feel like a

bus with 'Mammy' on the front – and the whole world was clambering on. Four women in a restaurant cheered when I ordered dessert. A friend went into a prolonged rage with me, for no reason at all. Everyone's unconscious was very close to their mouth. Whatever my pregnant body triggered was not social, or political, it was animal and ancient and quite help-less. It was also most unfair. Another friend showed me a pair of baby's shoes and said, 'Look, look!' He said that in prison, they show little shoes to child molesters to make them realise how small and vulnerable their victims were. He did not seem to notice that he had put pregnant women and child molesters in the same category, as if we both needed to be told what we were.

Perhaps he was right. A pregnant woman does not know what she is. She has been overtaken. She feels sick but she is not sick, she lives underwater, where there are no words. The world goes funny on her; it is accusing when she is delighted, and applauds when she feels like shit.

People without children went, without exception, a little mad. People who had children succumbed to a cherishing nostalgia. I began to enter into the romance of their lives, and see them as they must have been, newly married perhaps, and in love; dreaming of the future that they were living now. Pregnancy is a non-place, a suspension, a holiday from our fallible and compromised selves. There is no other time in a woman's life when she is so supported and praised and helped and loved. Though perhaps it is not 'she' who gets all the attention, but 'they'; this peculiar, mutant, double self – motherandchild.

I looked in the mirror. I had a body out of Rouault, big thick slabs of flesh, painted on stained glass. I was an amazement to myself, a work of engineering, my front cantilevered out from the solid buttress of my backside. Every night now, there was a ritual of wonder as we measured the bump. From week to week I felt my body shift into different cycles, like some slow-motion, flesh-based washing machine. 'Oh. Something else is happening now.' In the middle of January I surfaced, quite suddenly. I realised that the strenuous work was done, the baby was somehow 'made', all it had to do now was grow.

I have no idea why the first stages of pregnancy, when the child is so tiny, should be the most exhausting. I suppose you are growing your own cells before you start on theirs. Your blood volume goes up by 30 per cent, so your bone marrow is working, your very bone marrow is tired. It is as if you planted a seed and then had to build a field to grow it in. When that was over, everything, for me, was pure delight. If someone sold the hormones you get in the second trimester of pregnancy, I would become a junkie. I cycled everywhere, walked at a clip, fell asleep between one heartbeat and the next. I started dreaming again, vivid, intense, learning dreams. I was breast-feeding a blue-eyed girl and it was easy. I was in labour and it was easy – the child that slithered out was small and as hot as a childhood dream of wetting the bed; she was the precise temperature of flesh. Some of the dreams were funny, many were completely filthy. I had 30 per cent more blood in my body and, as far as I could tell, it was all going to the one place. Another thing the books don't tell you.

The child was still hiding. The days ticked inexorably past. I did not feel like an animal, I felt like a clock, one made of blood and bone, that you could neither hurry nor delay. At four and a half months, right on cue, it started to chime. Butterflies. A kick.

The child leapt in my womb. Actually, the child leaps in the womb all day long, but it takes time for the womb to realise it. You wait for the first kick but, like the first smile, the early versions are all 'just wind'. The first definite kick (which coincided with the discovery of the first, definite pile, a shock severe enough to send a surge of adrenalin through any child) was wonderful. My body had been blind, and I barely comprehending; I had begun to long for a sign, a little something in return. The first kick is the child talking back to you, a kind of softening up. I began to have ideas about this baby, even conversations with it, some of which, to my great embarrassment, took place out loud.

'Hello, sweetheart.'

Sugar made the child jump, as well as hunger. Music made it stop, a listening stillness. I began to time my digestion: ten minutes after chocolate, a kick; fifteen minutes after pasta; half an hour after meat. I was bounced awake at five every morning and got up for a bowl of cereal – already feeding this little tyrant, getting in training for the real event. Early afternoon was a cancan, also nine o'clock at night. I went to New York and the child stayed on Irish time, which was very odd. In the middle of the day I would go back to my hotel room for a rest and a chat. My belly made peculiar company. We watched *My Dinner with Andre* together, and ate big handfuls of nuts.

What did I know? I knew this child liked music, but maybe all children do. I thought it was an independent type, wriggling already, as though to get away. I began to identify whatever part of its body was squirming under my hand. One day a shoulder bone scything up from the depths, another day a little jutting heel. My indifference to the world grew vast. I liked things from a distance. I was in the middle of the sweetest, quietest romance.

In our first antenatal class the midwife said, 'Is there a pelvis over there on the floor behind you, could you pass it here?' And when some hapless male picked up the bit of dead person they used for demonstration purposes, she said, 'Don't be afraid of it. It's not a chalice.' I thought this was very Irish. Secretly, I thought that perhaps my pelvis *was* a chalice. I also thought that it might be beginning to crack. She passed around a vial of amniotic fluid (of unspecified age, it would have been nice to know if it was fresh) and on the other side of the room, a woman bent forward on to her belly, in an awkward, pregnant attempt at a faint. The midwife turned to a diagram – we had to have the window opened for air. She told us about perineal massage. I had never heard of anything so peculiar and unlikely in my life. I was surrounded by strangers, half of them men and all of them catatonic with shock. It might have been the way she lay down on a mat with her legs up in the air (she was in her late fifties), or it might just have been the fact that all of us realised that there was a fundamental problem, here, of design. The hole just wasn't big enough. And there was no escape now. I felt as though I had been watching a distant train for months and only now, when it was approaching, did I realise I was tied to the tracks.

My father says, quite wisely, that we should have been marsupials, pregnant up to six months, with the last three in a pouch. The disproportion was terrible. This could not be what nature intended, humans must be overbred. I couldn't walk for more than twenty minutes. Everything hurt. Somehow, I blamed the bump and not the child for the obstruction in my gut and the vile acid that was pushed up into my throat. We weren't

23

to take antacids, because they would make us anaemic, the midwife said. I said, 'What's so bad about anaemia?' thinking that it couldn't be worse than this. I sat and surfed the Net like some terrible turnip, gagging and leaning back in my chair. My shoes didn't fit. I became clumsy, and not just because of the weight out front – dishes dropped for no reason out of my hands. At thirty-five weeks, just like all the other women on the About.com pregnancy notice-board, I started fighting with Martin: even this was predetermined, as the hormonal conveyor belt ground on. Oh, the stupidity of it, the blankness, the sense-less days and the terrible, interrupted nights. Somewhere in there, I forgot entirely that I was having a child. Nothing wonderful could come of this. I was bored to madness, and there was nothing I, or anyone else, could do about it because I had the concentration span of a gnat. A very fat gnat.

The streets, that had been full of babies in their buggies, now became full of the old and the infirm, people who couldn't manage the step on to the bus, or who failed to reach the queue before the till closed. Was it possible that pregnancy was turning me into a nicer person? I thought of the women I knew when I was young who were pregnant all the time. I did sums: the mother of a school friend who had had twenty-two pregnancies, eleven of which had come to term. She would look up from her plate, surrounded by bottles of pills, and say, 'Oh . . . Hello . . .' as though trying to figure out if you had come out of her or someone else. Her husband was mad about her, you could still see it, and her children, with the exception of the eldest boys, were complete strangers.

Even my own much discussed, often caressed, high-focus bump was filled with someone I did not know. And perhaps never would. Pregnancy is as old-fashioned as religion, and it never ends. Every moment of my pregnancy lasted for ever. I was pregnant in the autumn, and I was pregnant in the spring. I was pregnant as summer came. I lived like a plant on the window-sill, taking its time, starting to bud. Nothing could hurry this. There was no technology for it: I was the technology – increasingly stupid, increasingly kind, a mystery to myself, to Martin, and to everyone who passed me by.

Birth

Amniotic fluid smells like tea. When I say this to Martin, he says, 'I thought that was just tea.' Of course a hospital should smell of tea: a hospital should smell of bleach. Unit C smells of tea and a little bit of ammonia, whether human or industrial is hard to tell. There is a lot of amniotic fluid in Unit C. At least three of the women have had their waters broken that afternoon, and as the evening approaches we sit draining into strips of unbleached cotton and watching each other, jealously, for signs of pain.

There is a little something extra in there, sharp and herbal – green tea maybe, or gunpowder tea. Pregnancy smelt like grass. Sort of. It certainly smelt of something growing; a distinctive and lovely smell that belongs to that family of grass, and ironed cotton, and asparagus pee. But the smell of tea is beginning to get to me. There are pints of it. I'm like some Burco Boiler with the tap left open. It flows slowly, but it will not stop. For hours I have been waiting for it to stop, and the mess of the bed is upsetting me. It upsets the housekeeper in me and it upsets the schoolgirl in me. The sanitary pads they hand you are school-issue and all the nurses are turning into nuns.

The breaking of the waters was fine. The nurse did whatever

magic makes sheets appear under you while other things are folded back, and the obstetrician did something deft with a crochet hook. There was the sense of pressure against a membrane, and then pop – a bit tougher but not much different from bursting a bubble on plastic bubble wrap. It felt quite satisfying, and the rush of hot liquid that followed made me laugh. I don't think a lot of women laugh at this stage in Unit C, but why not? We were on our way.

After which, there is nothing to do but wait. As the afternoon wears on, the pink curtains are pulled around the beds. The ward is full of breathing; the sharp intake of breath and the groaning exhalation, as though we are all asleep, or having sex in our sleep. One woman sobs behind her curtain. From the bed beside me the submarine sound of the Doppler looking for a foetal heartbeat and endlessly failing – a sonic rip as it is pulled away, then bleeping, breathing; the sigh and rush of an unseen woman's electronic blood.

Then there is tea. Actual tea. The men are sent out, for some reason, and the women sit around the long table in the middle of the ward. It's a school tea. There is a woman with high blood pressure, a couple of diabetics, one barely pregnant woman who has such bad nausea she has to be put on a drip. There are at least three other women on the brink, but they stay in bed and will not eat. I am all excited and want to talk. I am very keen to compare dressing-gowns – it took me so long to find this one, and I am quite pleased with it, but when I get up after the meal, the back of it is stained a watery red. I am beginning to hate Unit C.

After tea is the football. Portugal are playing France and, when a goal is scored, the men all come out from behind the curtains to watch the replay. Then they go back in again to their groaning, sighing women. I keep the curtain open and watch Martin while he watches the game. I am keeping track of my contractions, if they are contractions. At 9.35, Martin looks at me over the back of his chair. He gives me a thumbs-up as if to say, 'Isn't this a blast? And there's football on the telly!' At 9.35 and 20 seconds I am, for the first time, in serious pain. I am in a rage with him for missing it, and call to him quietly over the sound of the game.

A woman in a dressing-gown comes to talk to me. She is very big. I ask her if she is due tonight but she says she is not due until September, which is three months away. She is the woman from the next bed, the one with the Doppler machine. They couldn't find the foetal heartbeat because of the fat. She stands at the end of the bed and lists her symptoms, which are many. She has come up from Tipperary. She is going to have a Caesarean at thirty-one weeks. I am trying to be sympathetic, but I think I hate her. She is weakness in the room.

When I have a contraction I lurch out of bed, endlessly convinced that I have to go to the toilet – endlessly, stupidly convinced, every five minutes, that there is a crap I have to take, new and surprising as the first crap Adam took on his second day in the world. This journey to the toilet full of obstacles, the first one being Martin, whose patience is endless and whose feet are huge. When I get into the cubicle at the end of the ward, I sit uselessly on the toilet, try to mop up the mess, and listen to the woman on the other side of the partition, who is louder than me, and who doesn't seem to bother going back to her bed any more.

This has been happening, on and off, for a week. There is nothing inside me by way of food; there hasn't been for days. I am in what Americans call pre-labour, what the Irish are too macho to call anything at all. 'If you can talk through it, then it's not a contraction,' my obstetrician said when I came in a week ago, convinced that I was on my way. This week, she says, she will induce me because my blood pressure is up; but it may be simple charity. Ten days ago I wanted a natural birth, now I want a general anaesthetic. Fuck aromatherapy, I would do anything to make this stop – up to, and including, putting my head in the road, with my belly up on the kerb.

A woman answers her mobile, 'No, Ma, nothing yet. Stop calling! Nothing yet.' Pain overtakes the woman two beds down and the curtains are drawn. When they are pulled back, you can tell she is delighted. Oh, this is it. This *must* be it. Oh, oh, I'm going to have a baby. Then more pain – agony, it looks like. 'Oh, good girl! Good girl!' shouts the midwife, as the man collects her things and she is helped out of the Ante-Room to Hell that is Unit C. I am jealous, but I wish her well. The room is full of miracles waiting to happen, whether months or hours away. Another bed is empty – the woman on the other side of the toilet partition, is she in labour too? 'She went out, anyway,' says Martin. 'Hanging on to the wall.'

It is a theatre of pain. It is a pain competition (and I am losing). Martin says that Beckett would have loved Unit C. We wonder whether this is the worst place we have ever been, but decide that the prize still goes to the bus station in Nasca, the time we went to Peru and didn't bring any jumpers. All the paper pants I brought have torn and I sit knickerless on the unbleached sheet, which I have rolled up into a huge wad under me. My bump has shrunk a little, and gone slack. When I put my hand on it, there is the baby; very close now under the skin. I just know it is a girl. I feel her shoulder and an arm. For some reason I think of a skinned rabbit. I wonder are her

29

eyes open, and if she is waiting, like me. I have loved this child in a drowsy sort of way, but now I feel a big want in me for her, for this particular baby – the one that I am touching through my skin. 'Oh, when will I see you?' I say.

This could be the phrase of the night, but instead it is a song that repeats in my head. 'What sends her home hanging on to the wall? Boozin'! Bloody well boo-oozin'.' I stop getting out of bed every five minutes and start breathing, the way they told us to in the antenatal class. I count backwards from five when the pain hits, and then from five again. Was I in labour yet? Was this enough pain? 'If you can talk, then it's not labour.' So I try to keep talking, but by 11.00 the lights are switched off, I am lurching into sleep between my (non-)contractions for three or five minutes at a time, and Martin is nodding off in the chair.

My cervix has to do five things: it has to come forward, it has to shorten, it has to soften, it has to thin out, it has to open. A week earlier the obstetrician recited this list and told me that it had already done three of them. In the reaches of the night I try to remember which ones I have left to do, but I can't recall the order they come in, and there is always, as I press my counting fingers into the sheet, one that I have forgotten. My cervix, my cervix. Is it soft but not short? Is it soft and thin, but not yet forward? Is it short and hard, but open anyway? I have no sense that this is not a list but a sequence. I have lost my grasp of cause and effect. My cervix, my cervix: it will open as the clouds open, to let the sun come shining through. It will open like the iris of an eye, like the iris when you open the back of a camera. I could see it thinning; the tiny veins stretching and breaking. I could see it opening like something out of *Alien*. I could see it open as simply as a door that you don't know you've opened, until you are halfway across the room. I could see all this, but my cervix stayed shut.

At 2.30 a.m. I give in and Martin goes off to ask for some Pethidine. I know I will only be allowed two doses of this stuff, so it had better last a long time. I want to save the second for the birth, but in my heart of hearts I know I'm on my way to an epidural now. I don't know why I wanted to do without one, I suppose it was that Irishwoman machismo again. *Mná na hEireann. MNÁ na hEireann.* FIVE four three two . . . one. Fiiiive four three two one. Five. Four. Three. Two. One.

Once I give in and start to whimper, the (non-)contractions are unbearable. The Pethidine does not come. At 3 a.m. there is a shrieking from down the corridor, and I realise how close we are to the labour ward. The noise is ghastly, Victorian: it tears through the hospital dark. Someone is really giving it soprano. I think nothing of it. I do not wonder if the woman is mad, or if the baby has died, but that is what I wonder as I write this now.

Footsteps approach but they are not for me, they are for the woman from Tipperary who has started crying, with a great expenditure of snot, in the bed next door. The nurse comforts her. 'I'm just frikened,' the woman says. 'She just frikened me.' I want to shout that it's all right for her, she's going to have a fucking Caesarean, but it has been forty-five minutes since I realised that I could not do this any more, that the pain I had been riding was about to ride over me, and I needed something to get me back on top, or I would be destroyed by it, I would go under – in some spiritual and very real sense, I would die.

The footsteps go away again. They do not return. I look at Martin who is listening, as I am listening, and he disappears silently through the curtain. At 3.30 a.m., I get the Pethidine.

After this, I do not count through the (non-)contractions, or try to manage my breathing. I moan, with my mouth a little open. I *low*. I almost enjoy it. I sleep all the time now, between times. I have given in. I have untied my little boat and gone floating downstream.

At 5.00 a.m. a new woman comes along and tells Martin he must go home. There follows a complicated and slow conversation as I stand up to her (we are, after all, back in school). I say that I need him here, and she smiles, 'What for? What do you need him for?' (For saving me from women like you, *Missus*.) In the end, she tells us that there are mattresses he can sleep on in a room down the hall. Oh. Why didn't she say so? Maybe she's mad. It's 5 a.m., I'm tripping on Pethidine, at the raw end of a sleepless week, and this woman is a little old-fashioned, in a mad sort of way. Wow. We kiss. He goes. From now on, I stay under, not even opening my eyes when the pain comes.

I think I low through breakfast. They promise me a bed in the labour ward at 10.30, so I can stop lowing and start screaming, but that doesn't seem to be happening really. I am sitting up and smiling for the ward round, which is nice, but I am afraid that they will notice that the contractions are fading, and I'll have to start all over again, somehow. Then the contractions come back again, and by now my body is all out of Pethidine. I spend the minutes after 10.30 amused by my rage; astonished by how bad I feel. Are these the worst hundred seconds I have ever been through? How about the next hundred seconds – let's give them a go.

At 12.00, I nip into the cubicle for one last contraction, and we are out of Unit C. The whole ward lifts as we leave, wishing us well – another one on her way. I realise I have been lowing all night, keeping these women from sleep.

The room on the labour ward is extremely posh, with its own bathroom and a high-tech bed. I like the look of the midwife; she is the kind of woman you'd want to go for a few pints with. She is tired. She asks if I have a birth plan and I say I want to do everything as naturally as possible. She says, 'Well, you've made a good start, anyway,' which I think is possibly sarcastic, given the crochet hook, and the Pethidine, and the oxytocin drip they've just ordered up. Martin goes back to pack up our stuff, and I start to talk. She keeps a half-ironic silence. For months, I had the idea that if I could do a bit of research, get a bit of chat out of the midwife, then that would take my mind off things – what is the worst thing that anyone ever said? or the weirdest? – but she won't play ball. I run out of natter and have a little cry. She says, 'Are you all right?' I say, 'I just didn't think I would ever get this far, that's all.' And I feel her soften behind me.

I don't remember everything that followed, but I do remember the white, fresh light. I also remember the feelings in the room. I could sense a shift in mood, or intention, in the women who tended me, with great clarity. It was like being in a painting. Every smile mattered; the way people were arranged in the space, the gestures they made.

I have stopped talking. The midwife is behind me, arranging things on a stand. Martin is gone, there is silence in the room. She is thinking about something. She isn't happy. It is very peaceful.

Or: She tries to put in the needle for the drip. Martin is on my right-hand side. I seem to cooperate but I won't turn my hand around. The stain from the missed vein starts to spread and she tries again. I am completely uninterested in the pain from the needle.

Or: A woman walks in, looks at me, glances between my legs. 'Well done!' she says, and walks back out again. Perhaps she just walked into the wrong room.

Even at a low dose, the oxytocin works fast. It is bucking through my system, the contractions gathering speed: the donkey who is kicking me is getting really, really annoyed. The midwife goes to turn up the drip and I say, 'You're not touching that until I get my epidural.' A joke.

A woman puts her head round the door, then edges into the room. She says something to the midwife, but they are really talking about something else. She half-turns to me with a smile. There is something wrong with one of the blood tests. She tells me this, then she tells the midwife that we can go ahead anyway. The midwife relaxes. I realise that, sometimes, they don't give you an epidural. Even if you want one. They just can't. Then everyone has a bad morning.

The midwife goes to the phone. Martin helps to turn me on my side. The contractions now are almost continuous. Within minutes, a woman in surgical greens walks in. 'Hi!' she says. 'I'm your pain-relief consultant.' She reaches over my bare backside to shake my hand. This is a woman who loves her job. Martin cups my heels and pushes my knees up towards my chest, while she sticks the needle in my spine, speaking clearly and loudly, and working at speed. I am bellowing by now, pretty much. FIVE, I roar (which seems to surprise them – five what?) FOUR. THREE. (Oh, good woman! That's it!) TWO. One. FIVE. They hold me like an animal that is trying to kick free, but I am not – I am doing this, I am getting this done. When it is over, the anaesthetist breaks it to me that it might be another ten minutes before I feel the full effect. I do not have ten minutes to spare, I want to tell her this, but fortunately, the pain has already begun to dull.

The room turns to me. The anaesthetist pats down her gown and smiles. She is used to the most abject gratitude, but I thank the midwife instead, for getting the timing spot on. The woman who talked about my blood tests has come back and the midwife tells me that she is finishing up now, Sally will see me through. This is a minor sort of betrayal, but I feel it quite keenly. Everyone leaves. Martin goes for a sandwich and Sally runs ice-cubes up my belly to check the line of the epidural. There is no more pain.

Sally is lovely: sweetness itself. She is the kind of woman who is good all the way through. It is perhaps 1.30 and in the white light, with no pain, I am having the time of my life. Literally. Karen, the obstetrician, tells me my cervix has gone from practically 0 to 8 centimetres, in no time flat. The heavens have opened, the sun has come shining through. Martin is called back from the canteen. He watches the machines as they register the pain that I cannot feel any more. He says the contractions are off the scale now. We chat a bit and have a laugh, and quite soon Sally says it is time to push. Already.

For twenty hours women have been telling me I am wonderful, but I did not believe them until now. I know how to do this, I have done it in my dreams. I ask to sit up a bit and the bed rises with a whirr. Martin is invited to 'take a leg' and he politely accepts, 'Oh, thank you.' Sally takes the other one, and braces it – my shin against her ribs. Push! They both lean into me. I wait for the top of the contraction, catch it, and ride the wave. I can feel the head, deliciously large under my pubic bone. I can feel it as it eases further down. I look at Martin, all the while – here is a present for you, mister, this one is for you – but he is busy watching the business end. Karen is back, and they are all willing me on like football hooligans, Go on! Go on! One more now, and Push! Good woman! Good girl! I can hear the knocking of the baby's hearbeat on the foetal monitor, and the dreadful silence as I push. Then, long before I expect it, Sally says, 'I want you to pant through this one. Pant.' The child has come down, the child is there. Karen says, Yes, you can see the head. I send Martin down to check the colour of the hair. (A joke?) Another push. I ask may I touch, and there is the top of the head, slimy and hot and – what is most terrifying – soft. Bizarrely, I pick up Martin's finger to check that it is clean, then tell him he must feel how soft it is. So he does. After which – enough nonsense now – it is back to pushing. Sally reaches in with her flat-bladed scissors and Martin, watching, lets my leg go suddenly slack. We are mid-push. I kick out, and he braces against me again. Karen, delighted, commands me to, 'Look down now, and see your baby being born.' I tilt my head to the maximum; and there is the back of the baby's head, easing out beyond my belly's horizon line. It is black and red, and wet. On the next push, machine perfect, it slowly turns. And here it comes – my child; my child's particular profile. A look of intense concentration, the nose tilted up, mouth and eyes tentatively shut. A blind man's face, vivid with sensation. On the next push, Sally catches the shoulders and lifts the baby out and up – in the middle of which movement the mouth opens, quite simply, for a first breath. It simply starts to breathe.

'It's a girl!'

Sally says afterwards that we were very quiet when she came out. But I didn't want to say the first thing that came to mind

36

– which was, 'Is it? Are you sure?' A newborn's genitals are swollen and red and a bit peculiar looking, and the cord was surprisingly grey and twisted like a baroque pillar. Besides, I was shy. How to make the introduction? I think I eventually said, 'Oh, I knew you would be,' I think I also said, 'Oh, come here to me, darling.' She was handed to me, smeared as she was with something a bit stickier than cream cheese. I laid her on my stomach and pulled at my T-shirt to clear a place for her on my breast. She opened her eyes for the first time, looking into my face, her irises cloudy. She blinked and found my eyes. It was a very suspicious, grumpy look, and I was devastated.

Martin, doing the honours at a festive dinner, cut the cord. After I pushed out the placenta, Karen held it up for inspection, twirling it on her hand like a connoisseur: a bloody hairnet, though heavier and more slippy.

The baby was long. Her face looked like mine. I had not prepared myself for this: this really astonished me. 'She looks like me.' And Martin said (an old joke), 'But she's got my legs.' At some stage, she was wrapped rigid in a blue blanket, which was a mercy, because I could hardly bear the smallness of her. At some stage, they slipped out, leaving us to say, 'Oh, my God,' a lot. I put her to a nipple and she suckled. 'Oh, my *God*,' said Martin. I looked at him as if to say, 'Well, what did you expect?' I rang my mother who said, 'Welcome to the happiest day of your life,' and started to cry. I thought this was a little over the top. In a photograph taken at this time, I look pragmatic and unsurprised, as though I had just cleaned the oven and was about to tackle the fridge.

I am not stricken until they wheel us down to the ward. The child looks at the passing scene with alert pleasure. She is so clear and sharp. She is saturated with life, she is intensely alive. Her face is a little triangle and her eyes are shaped like leaves, and she looks out of them, liking the world.

Two hours later I am in the shower. When I clean between my legs I am surprised to find everything numb and mushy. I wonder why that is. Then I remember that a baby's head came out of there, actually came out. When I come to, I am sitting on a nurse. She is sitting on the toilet beside the shower. The shower is still going. I am very wet. She is saying, 'You're all right, you're all right, I've got you.' I think I am saying, 'I just had a baby. I just had a baby,' but I might be trying to say it, and not saying anything at all.

Milk

The milk surprises me. It does not disgust me as much as I thought it would, unless it is not fresh. It is disturbing that a piece of you should go off so quickly. I don't think Freud ever discussed lactation, but the distinction between 'good' and 'bad' bodily products here is very fine. Women leak so much. Perhaps this is why we clean – which is to say that a man who cleans is always 'anal', a woman who cleans is just a woman.

There certainly is a lot of it, and it gets everywhere, and the laundry is a fright. But what fun! to be granted a new bodily function so late in life. As if you woke up one morning and could play the piano. From day to day the child is heavier in your arms, she plumps up from wrist to ankle, she has dimples where her knuckles were, she has fat on her toes. I thought we might trade weight, pound for pound, but she is gaining more than I am losing. I am faced with bizarre and difficult calculations – the weight of the groceries in a bag versus the weight of her nappies in a bag. Or my weight, plus a pint of water, minus four ounces of milk, versus her weight, plus four ounces, divided by yesterday. When I was at school, a big-chested friend put her breasts on the scales and figured that they weighed 2 pounds each. I don't know how she did it, but I still think that she was wrong. Heavier. Much heavier.

It is quite pleasant when a part of your body makes sense, after many years. A man can fancy your backside, but you still get to sit on it; breasts, on the other hand, were always just there. Even so, the anxiety of pregnancy is the anxiety of puberty all over again. I am thirty-seven. I don't want my body to start 'doing' things, like some kind of axolotl. I do not believe people when they say these things will be wonderful, that they are 'meant'. I am suspicious of the gleam in women's eyes, that pack of believers, and listen instead to the voice of a friend who breast-fed her children until they were twenty-eight and a half, and who now says, 'They're like ticks.'

So I feed the child because I should, and resign myself to staying home. I never liked being around nursing women – there was always too much love, too much need in the room. I also suspected it to be sexually gratifying. For whom? Oh, for everyone: for the mother, the child, the father, the father-in-law. Everyone's voice that little bit nervy, as though it weren't happening: everyone taking pleasure in a perv-lite middle-class sort of way. Ick. 'The only women who breast-feed are doctors' wives and tinkers,' a friend's mother was told forty years ago, by the nurse who delivered her. I thought I sensed a similar distaste in the midwives, a couple of months ago, who were obliged by hospital and government policy to prod the child and pinch my nipple, though perhaps – let's face it, sisters – not quite that hard. It is probably easier for men, who like breasts in general, but I have always found them mildly disgusting, at least up close. They also often make me jealous. Even the word 'breast' is difficult. Funny how many people say they find public breast-feeding a bit 'in your face'. Oh, the rage.

So, let us call it 'nursing' and let us be discreet – it is still the best way I know to clear a room. My breast is not the problem (left, or right, whichever is at issue), the 'problem' is the noise. Sometimes the child drinks as simply as from a cup, other times she snorts and gulps, half-drowns, sputters and gasps; then she squawks a bit, and starts all over again. This may be an iconised activity made sacred by some and disgusting by others, but it is first and foremost a meal. It is only occasionally serene. It also takes a long time. I do smile at her and coo a bit, but I also read a lot (she will hate books), talk, or type (this, for example). Afterwards she throws up. People stare at the whiteness of it, as I did at first. Look. Milk.

'It was the whiteness of the whale that above all appalled me.' The nineteenth century took their breasts very seriously, or so I suspect – I can't really get into a library to check. I am thinking of those references I found particularly exciting or unsettling as a child. The heroes of *King Solomon's Mines*, for example, as they toil up Sheba's left Breast (a mountain) suffering from a torturing thirst. The chapter is called 'Water Water!' and comes from a time when you were allowed to be so obvious it hurt. 'Heavens, how we did drink!' These extinct volcanoes are 'inexpressibly solemn and overpowering' and difficult to describe. They are wreathed about with 'strange mists and clouds [that] gathered and increased around them, till presently we could only trace their pure and gigantic outline swelling ghostlike through the fleecy envelope'. In a desperate drama of hunger and satiation our heroes climb through lava and snow up to the hillock of the enormous, freezing nipple. There they find a cave, occupied by a dead man (what?! what?!), and in this cave one of their party also dies: Ventvogel, a 'hottentot' whose 'snub-nose' had, when he was alive, the ability to sniff out water (we don't want to know).

So far, so infantile. I watch the child's drama at the breast, and (when I am not reading, typing, or talking) cheer her along. She wakes with a shout in the middle of the night, and I wonder at her dreams; there is a dead man in a cave, perhaps, somewhere about my person. Oh, dear. When did it all get so serious? I turn to Swift for the comedy, as opposed to tragedy, of scale, but Gulliver perched on a Brobdingnagian nipple turns out, on rereading, to be part of a great disgustfest about giant women pissing. None of this seems *true* to me. I have no use for the child's disgust, as she has no use for mine. I am besotted by a being who is, at this stage, just a set of emotions arranged around a gut. Who is just a shitter, who is just a soul.

Are all mothers Manicheans? This is just one of the hundreds of questions that have never been asked about motherhood. What I am interested in is not the drama of being a child, but this new drama of being a mother (yes, there are cannibals in my dreams, yes) about which so little has been written. Can mothers not hold a pen? Or is it just the fact that we are all children, when we write?

I go to Books Upstairs in Dublin, to find a poem by Eavan Boland. The child in the stroller is ghetto fabulous in a white babygro complete with hoodie. I am inordinately, sadly proud of the fact that she is clean. We negotiate the steps, we knock over some books. The child does a spectacular crap in the silence of the shop, in front of the section marked 'Philosophy'. I say, 'Oh, look at all the books. Oh, *look* at all the books,' because I believe in talking to her, and I don't know what else to say.

The poem is called 'Night Feed' and is beautifully measured

and very satisfying: 'A silt of milk. / The last suck. / And now your eyes are open, / Birth coloured and offended.'

But the poet chooses a bottle not a breast, placing the poem in the bland modernity of the suburbs. I grew up in those suburbs. I know what we were running away from. Because the unpalatable fact is that the Ireland of my childhood had the closest thing to a cow cult outside of India. When I was eleven, I won a Kodak Instamatic camera in the Milk Competition, a major annual event, when every school child in the country had to write an essay called 'The Story of Milk'. I can still remember the arrival of the Charolais cattle, which marked the beginning of Ireland's love affair with Europe. The most exciting thing about economic union, for my farming relatives, was not the promise of government grants but this big-eyed, nougat-coloured breed of bull whose semen could be used in beef or dairy herds – as good, if you will pardon the phrase, for meat as for milk. It was a romantic animal, as hopeful as the moon shot. There were cuff-links made in the shape of the Charolais and men wore them to Mass and to the mart. And the romance lingers on. A couple of years ago, a media personality of my acquaintance bought four of them, to match her curtains.

The country was awash with milk. Kitchens and bedrooms were hung with pictures of the Madonna and child. After the arrival of infant formula in the fifties, breast-feeding became more of a chosen, middle-class activity, but it was still common in the countryside, and was everywhere practised as a fairly optimistic form of contraception. Still, though general all over Ireland, breast-feeding was absolutely hidden. The closest the culture came to an image of actual nursing was in the icon of the Sacred Heart, endlessly offering his male breast, open and glowing, and crowned with thorns.

43

Actually, you know, breast-feeding hurts. Certainly, at first, it really fucking hurts. On the third night of my daughter's life I was left with a human being the size of a cat and nothing to sustain her with but this *stub*. Madwomen (apparently) think that their babies are possessed. And they are. They look at you, possessed by their own astonishing selves. You say, Where did that come from? You say, Where did YOU come from? This baby is pure need – a need you never knew you had. And all you have to offer is a mute part of your body which, you are told, will somehow start 'expressing', as though it might start singing 'Summertime'. You feed your child, it seems, on hope alone. There is nothing to see. You do not believe the milk exists until she throws it back up, and when she does, you want to cry. What is not quite yours as it leaves you, is definitely yours as it comes back.

So there we were in the hospital dark; me and my white Dracula, her chin running with milk and her eyes black. What I remember is how fully human her gaze was, even though it was so new. She seemed to say that this was a serious business, that we were in it together. Tiny babies have such emotional complexity. I am amazed that 'bravery' is one of the feelings she has already experienced, that she should be born so intrepid and easily affronted, that she should be born so much herself.

She is also, at this early stage, almost gender free. This is useful. The statistics on how much less girl babies are breast-fed, as opposed to boys, are shocking. There are probably a number of reasons for this, but one of them surely is the degree to which our society has sexualised the breast. All in all, sex has ruined breast-feeding. It is a moral business these days – a slightly dirty, slightly wonderful, always unsettling, duty. It has

44

no comic aspects. No one has told the child this: she seems to find it, finally, quite amusing – as indeed do I.

We turn to Sterne to find glee, envy, all those ravening eighteenth-century emotions, transmuted by language into delight. Shandy quotes Ambrose Paraeus on the stunting effect of the nursing breast on a child's nose, particularly those 'organs of nutrition' that have 'firmness and elastic repulsion'. These were 'the undoing of the child, inasmuch as his nose was so snubb'd, so rebuff'd, so rebated, and so refrigerated thereby, as never to arrive ad mensuram suam legitimam'. What was needed was a soft, flaccid breast so that, 'by sinking into it . . . as into so much butter, the nose was comforted, nourish'd, plump'd up, refresh'd, refocillated, and set a growing for ever'.

This was still when 'breast' was a common, easy word. Men placed their hands on their breasts, had pistols pointed at them, and were in general so set to a-swelling and a-glowing as to put the girls to shame. There is a distinction between 'breast' and 'breasts', of course, but it is still charming to think that this seat of honesty and sentiment is the singular of a plural that provoked desire. As if, in modern terms, we got horny watching someone's eyes fill with tears. As, indeed, sometimes, we do.

No. The milk surprises me, above all, because it hurts as it is let down, and this foolish pain hits me at quite the wrong times. The reflex is designed to work at the sight, sound, or thought of your baby – which is spooky enough – but the brain doesn't seem to know what a baby *is*, exactly, and so tries to make you feed anything helpless, or wonderful, or small. So I have let down milk for Russian submariners and German tourists dying on Concorde. Loneliness and technology get me every time, get my milk every time. Desire, also, stabs me not in the heart but on either side of the heart – but I had expected this. What I had not expected was that there should be some things that do not move me, that move my milk. Or that, sometimes, I only realise that I am moved when I feel the pain. I find myself lapsed into a memory I cannot catch, I find myself trying to figure out what it is in the room that is sad or lovely – was it that combination of words, or the look on his face? – what it is that has such a call on my unconscious attention, or my pituitary, or my alveolar cells.

There is a part of me, I have realised, that wants to nurse the stranger on the bus. Or perhaps it wants to nurse the bus itself, or the tree I see through the window of the bus, or the child I once was, paying my fare on the way home from school. This occasional incontinence is terrifying. It makes me want to shout – I am not sure what. Either, Take it! or, Stop! If the world would stop needing then my body would come back to me. My body would come home.

I could ask (in a disingenuous fashion) if this is what it is like to be bothered by erections. Is this what it is like to be bothered by tears? Whatever – I think we can safely say that when we are moved, it is some liquid that starts moving: blood, or milk, or salt water. I did not have a very tearful pregnancy, mostly because we don't have a television. Pregnant women cry at ads for toilet tissue: some say it is the hormones, but I think we have undertaken such a great work of imagining, we are prone to wobble on the high wire. Of course, the telly has always been a provoker of second-hand tears as well as second-hand desire. Stories, no matter how fake, produce a real biological response in us, and we are used to this. But the questions my nursing body raises are more testing to me. Do we need stories in order to produce emotion, or is an emotion already a story? What is the connection, in other words, between narrative and my alveolar cells?

I suspect, as I search the room for the hunger by the fire-place, or the hunger in her cry, that I have found a place before stories start. Or the precise place where stories start. How else can I explain the shift from language that has happened in my brain? This is why mothers do not write, because motherhood happens in the body, as much as the mind. I thought child-birth was a sort of journey that you could send dispatches home from, but of course it is not – it *is* home. Everywhere else now, is 'abroad'.

A child came out of me. I cannot understand this, or try to explain it. Except to say that my past life has become foreign to me. Except to say that I am prey, for the rest of my life, to every small thing.

Damn.

Nine Months

Day One: Ah

Development (the baby)
I wake up to the sound of my baby saying, 'Ah.' It is the morning after she was born. 'Ah.' She says it clear and true. This is her voice. It sounds slightly surprised at itself. It certainly surprises me. 'Ah.' There she goes again.

Perhaps it is a reflex, the way this baby will stride across the sheet when you set her feet on the bed. She already knows how to talk, but it will be some months before she stops teasing me, and does it again.

We are born knowing everything.

Regression (me)
I wake up to the sound of my baby saying, 'Ah.' It is the morning after she was born. 'Ah.' She says it clear and true. This is her voice. It sounds slightly surprised at itself. It certainly surprises me. 'Ah.' There she goes again.

She should be crying, but she is talking instead; experimenting with this sound that comes out of her mouth. The womb is so silent. And of course. Of course! It is obvious! I have given birth to a perfect child.

I look into the cot and watch for a while. Then I decide that I must have another baby immediately.

You see, I never believed, until just this moment, that I could do this, that it could be done. Now I know that it is true – something as simple as sex can make something as complicated as a baby, a real one, and I think, What a great trick! and I wonder, How soon? How soon can we do the impossible again?

It is now the end of June. With a bit of luck we can start again in the middle of August. We could have another one by . . . next May. Allow three months for trying and failing – latest, I'll be in labour again by August of next year. Which means that I'll have to write that novel in five months, proofs at Christmas, to rush for publication late spring, and then, pop, another baby! Perfect. It all fits. I have to ring Martin and tell him this. I pick up the mobile phone he has left for me by the bedside and I dial a three. I cancel and try a six. I cancel again. I can't remember our phone number.

Usually, it takes me three years to write a book, but that's no problem: I can make babies, for heaven's sake, novels are a doddle. Look, it is all there in my head. I can flick through the pages and know the shape of it: I can relish the tone.

The novel is in my head but the phone number is not in my head. I look around the room and have a think. It's in my file – of course it is. There: just under my name. I follow the numbers with my finger and dial.

I used to be good at numbers. My brain must have been reconfigured during the night, somehow. I had heard that motherhood makes you stupid, maybe this is what they meant. Never mind, I can always use a phone book. I can do anything. I can conceive a child in the middle of November, say the 12th or 13th – Is that mid-week? It would probably be more relaxed if I ovulated at a weekend. I must ask Martin to get down the calendar.

He answers the phone.

The First Month: Dream-time

Development (the baby)

We dream, in our first weeks, more than at any other time in our lives. More than all the rest of our dreams over the whole span of our days. Constant dreaming. I wonder if she knows that she is awake. She opens her eyes and the world is there, she closes them and it is still there – or something very like it: the long shift of light and darkness that is week one, week two, week three. The landscape of her mother's breast. The earth-quake of her mother's rising out of bed. The noise of it all.

Two faces. Two people grinning, singing, cooing, calling to her. They gaze into her eyes – but *deep* into her eyes and they do not look away. They smile – a massive break in the O of the face. Hello. Yes. Hello. Something blanks out in her head and she turns away.

Overload. Shut-down.

Regression (me)

I never feel her skin. She is always dressed – another vest, another babygro, always snowy white, then yellowing at the neck from crusted milk. I change her all the time, but bit by bit. I change the nappy and then the vest. Nothing will persuade me to give her a bath. She has no fat yet, under this skin of hers. So much of what we think of as skin, the pleasure of it, the way it runs under our fingers, is actually fat. Merciful, sweet fat.

I was looking forward to the softness of her, and I thought her skin would look so new. But it looks as though it belongs to someone who has been in the bath too long. It is too thin. Seven layers of cells, that is what I remember from school – our surface is seven cells thick. But I think she has only three or four. I think she has only one. It is not so much a skin, as a glaze.

At the weekend, in my parents' house, my mother quite tactfully clears the room. Just in time. I weep like someone who has been in a car crash. I weep like someone who has woken up from a dream, to find that is all true, after all.

'Have a good cry,' says my mother, for the first time in twenty-five years. She too, at last, on home ground.

The Second Month

Development (the baby)
The books (the books!) say that her hands will uncurl this month, but they have always been open. Open and large and long. On the day she was born, her father looked at them and said, in a deeply regretful way, 'You know we're going to have to get a piano, now.'

She lies on her back on the white bed, wearing a white babygro, and she twists her hands slowly in front of her face; utterly graceful. She does it when there is music playing, looking very ancient, and centred, and Chinese.

She still sleeps, most of the time.

The baby wakes with a yelp of hunger, and she goes for the breast like a salty old dog. 'Aaarh,' goes her mouth, as she roots to one side. 'Aaarh.' She turns away from it to fill a nappy – which is serious work, of permanently uncertain outcome, or so it seems to her; always surprising, and bravely undertaken.

'Oh, good girl!'

We squeak toys on her tummy and smile, before she blanks out, or closes her eyes to sleep again. And then one day, she does not blank out. She smiles.

Regression (me)

I am still not walking so well and the blood is an absolute nuisance. I look up the Internet to try and find someone who knows when this is supposed to stop, but it's all about joy and despair, it's all feeding and postnatal depression and not a single thing about leakage, seepage, anaemia. Never mind.

In the first weeks, some book tells me, I am supposed to take three baths a day. Hah! I run a bath and the water goes cold before I have a chance to get into it. I sit in a bath and then lurch like a big wet cow out of the bath, carefully, carefully over the tiles, to run to the baby. What does the baby want? We are all agreed that this is a very contented baby, but it seems, all the same, that ten minutes away from this contented baby is one minute too many. Here, darling, here's your big, wet Ma.

Actually I don't mind the bath so much, a quick dip is fine, I don't really need clean hair. I can't go out anyway, because my feet are still too big for all my shoes, except for one pair of floppy, disgusting sneakers. I don't mind that either. If I made a list of the things I cannot do, it would start and finish with going to the toilet. I never thought of going to the toilet as a fundamental human right, but I do now. It should be in some UN Charter, the opportunity and the privacy, the biological ability to go to the toilet. No one mentions this on the Internet. They talk about sex instead. Sex. Crikey.

At the recommended time, we try a bit of sex. It's a wasteland down there. Women are awful liars. I do not think of all the women who gave birth in pain any more, I think of all the women who conceived in pain; the Irish families with eleven months between one child and the next. Did they feel the way I do, now – and then get pregnant again? No wonder they didn't tell us anything – those lowered voices in the kitchen when I was a child. Welcome to the big secret – it hurts.

But I really cannot believe that it hurts like this for everyone. Maybe I am too old. Maybe it is the fact that I have very loose joints. I think it isn't the tissue that hurts so much as the bones.

I don't know. I have never heard anyone discussing how long the pain is supposed to last. So I draw upon however many ghastly generations of suffering have preceded me and when I go back for my check-up, I smile hugely and say that everything is fine, wonderful, marvellous. I don't want to piss on the parade, and besides, it is true: I am extravagantly happy – messy, creaky, bewildered, exhausted, and in pain, but happy, hopeful, and immensely refreshed by it all.

Meanwhile, Martin is still on paternity leave and I can sleep. I have a talent for it. I doze, I nap, I snooze. I have no problem doing this. For the first time in months, I have an easy dream life – it seems my unconscious has relaxed. If the baby cries, on the other hand, I shoot up in the bed like an electrocuted corpse. Never mind the empty husk of your discarded body – pregnancy doesn't stop once they are out. I am still attached to this baby, I still feed myself in order to feed her. The only difference is the distance between us, now – all that space and air to get through. Air that she can suck in, and then exhale.

The baby cries. She cries on Saturday and also on Sunday. She does not take a break on Sunday night. And on Monday morning she cries again. We become acquainted with the long reaches of the night.

There are two, exactly opposite, ways to describe all this, and so I start to train myself in. The baby is a happy baby, I say, and lo! it is true. If I said the opposite, then this would become true instead. The baby is cranky, we will never sleep again – I would spiral downwards and the baby (the family! the house!) would be dragged down with me. So the baby is a happy baby because we have no other option, and the more we say it, the more true it becomes.

Besides. Look.

Such a beautiful, beautiful baby.

Once, maybe twice a day, I get an image of terrible violence against the baby. Like a flicker in the corner of my eye, it lasts for a quarter of a second, maybe less. Sometimes it is me who inflicts this violence, sometimes it is someone else. Martin says it is all right – it is just her astonishing vulnerability that works strange things in my head. But I know it is also because I am trapped, not just by her endless needs, but also by the endless, mindless love I have for her. It is important to stay on the right side of a love like this. For once, I am glad I am an older mother. I don't panic. I put a limit on the images that flash across my mind's eye. I am allowed two per day, maybe three. If I get more than that, then it's off to the doctor for the happy pills. Shoes or no shoes.

The Third Month

Development (the baby)
The baby cries for three days, on and off, and then she does something new, or she does a number of new things, all at once. She starts to grab and she also discovers her mouth, running her tongue around her lips. Or she finds her toes and starts to babble, both at the same time. The crying stops.

I wonder what was happening, for those three days? Waking up and crying, or turning and crying – seeing, reaching, scrabbling and suddenly setting up a wail. Brain fever. Hints and premonitions. Her mind is pulling itself up by its own bootstraps. There is something she must do, and she does not know what it is. Something is within reach, and she does not know what it might be. She has never done any of this before, and yet she knows that she has to do it. The shift and pressure of it must be huge. And then, all of a sudden, she breaks through. Not only 'habwabwa' but also toes! Not only this, but the other thing!

So that's what it was. What a relief.

Babies always know they have achieved something. They are naturally proud of themselves. She has a new expression every day now. Her worried look is more worried, her smile is slow, and complex, and huge.

Regression (me)
Somewhere in this month I realise that the baby will live, that when I wake up she will still be breathing.

From one day to the next, she changes from a tiny, mewling creature into the proper baby she is. All those old-fashioned words now apply: bonny, dandle, gurgle, dimple, posset. I give in to my stubbornly large feet, and buy new shoes.

I walk the streets of Dublin with the baby in a sling and everyone smiles at me and at my child. 'Isn't he lovely?' they say, assuming, for some reason, it is a boy. A man leans towards me on the bus. 'It's very hot,' he says. 'I have some water, ma'am, if you'd like to sponge the baby down.'

At home, Martin puts on her babygro, limb by tiny limb. 'Where did Napoleon put his armies?' he says. 'In his sleevies!'

I watch them and think how impossible it all is. I cannot see how this baby will grow into a person, any old person – a person like you, or me, or your boss, or that middle-aged woman in the street. I cannot see where it all goes.

The Fourth Month

Development (the baby)
The baby is becoming herself. Every day she is more present to us. A personality rises to the surface of her face, like a slowly developing Polaroid. She frowns for the first time, and it looks quite comical – the deliberate, frowny nature of her frown.

Or maybe she is disappearing. There was something so essential about her when she was just a tiny scrap: something astonishing and tenacious and altogether herself.

The baby disappears into her own personality. She gets rounder. Her features begin to look strangely confined, like a too-small mask in the middle of her big, round face.

It is now that babies look like Queen Victoria or Winston Churchill, or anyone fat, and British, and in charge. She is most imperious when her father picks her up. She sits in his arms and looks over at me as if to say, So who are you?

Regression (me)

The baby sits in her father's arms and looks over at me, like I am a stranger, walked in off the street. Oh, that blank stare. It makes me laugh, and go over to her, and take her back from him.

Silly baba.

When I have her safe, I look at Martin, and sometimes I recognise the wan feeling that men get, after a baby is born.

I spend the next while renegotiating this new, triangular love, with its lines of affection and exclusion. I try to make it whole. The thing I have to remember is that love is, in general, a good thing (though it often feels terrible, to me). I can see why people panic about all this: they panic about their partners being lost to them, or they panic about their babies being lost to them. Men, mostly – but not just men. Whoever is most the child in the relationship is the one who is most displaced.

I think that means me.

So, for a while I try to be, and am, that 'Mother' thing – the one who holds everyone, even myself, and keeps us safe. The container (the old bag, my dear, the old bag).

The Fifth Month

Development (the baby)

The baby looks, not at her fluffy toys' faces, eyes, ears or bits of ribbon, but at the label stitched into a seam. They all have one – a big disproportional loop of washing instructions and warnings about flammability. She likes the intricacy of the writing, but perhaps in an endlessly variable world, she is attracted to something constant and small. So much for her blue heffalump with the red feet, so much for her squeaky pink mouse – let's stick to Surface Wash Only, and the importance of 40 degrees.

Regression (me)

We bring the baby to America, on a book tour. Feeding her in a coffee shop, changing her nappy on the side of the road. Everywhere I travel, I think of refugees, and all the millions of women with babies in their arms, desperate for the next safe place. There is a sixteen-year-old girl in Bosnia who lives in my head, and she is doing this job just as well as I am, with as much tenderness and as much fear.

The book tour goes all right. I think.

I fly to Toronto and the baby goes home with her father. It doesn't occur to me to feel guilty. I drink my head off. I lactate a little mournfully into hotel sinks and make jokes about Baileys Irish Cream. I have a brilliant time (and I walk back in the door shaking like a lover).

Finished feeding, I go back on the cigarettes. I am addicted to nicotine, but I am also addicted to slipping away for two minutes every hour, and being alone. Just two minutes, maybe three. The cigarettes are in a closed room, and the ashtray is beside my computer. When she is asleep, I work. I think I am becoming addicted to working, too.

I am amazed at how much I have done. The baby sleeps for hours at a time, and I can't exactly leave the flat. So I might as well sit and type. All kinds of stuff. It doesn't look stupid to me – maybe that comes later, after you spend a few thousand hours saying, 'Look at the BLUE balloon.' So I write even faster, to outrun my fate.

The baby sleeps, and I am free. I have not so much left the

human race, as just left the *race* – which suits my kind of work very well. I feel sorry for all the parents who earn their money in the real world and have to go back out there again. If you spend a few months away from the game – the shopping, shagging, striving game – then it must be hard to see the point of it, quite.

I start a short story, a woman who says, '*There is a lull, a sort of hopelessness that comes over women just before they have children, or so it was with me. I did not know where it came from. Perhaps it came from my body, perhaps it came from my life, but I had the feeling that what I was doing was no good, or that I was no good at it. I have seen other women sink suddenly like this, they lose confidence, they dither, and then, shortly afterwards, they have children.*'

Is this true?

The child sleeps. I write about a woman on a ship, with a baby in her belly. Travelling on.

The Sixth Month

Development (the baby)
The baby has discovered locomotion (and frustration), propelling herself on her nappied bum, on her back, across the room. I experience dread. I cannot bring the toy to her, I cannot help her to the toy. There is a lot of grunting. I wait until it reaches a certain pitch, and give in.

She is no sooner in my arms than she is scrabbling around to reach whatever thing I have not noticed was there in the first place. The world is chock-full of ignored objects, for which the baby has no filter. A discarded CD case, a packet of seeds, a tweezers, a notebook. I am worn out and amazed by her constant ambient, grazing attention, as she flings herself from me to get at one thing or another, obliging me to catch her, time and again. The world is a circus and I am her trapeze, her stilts, her net. Not just mother, also platform and prosthesis. I'm not sure I feel like a person, any more.

I think I feel a little used.

Regression (me)

In the run-up to Christmas we take the baby out, and everyone says she is the image of her father. 'I'm not a woman,' I say, 'I'm a photocopier.' But Martin is delighted to have a little version of himself, spookily female, in his arms. When I complain, he laughs and says, 'You were just the venue.'

I am a cheap drunk. Two glasses of mulled wine and I am completely squiffy, going around the room asking, 'When does the sex thing, you know . . . get back on track?' I am conducting a straw poll. I ask the men, because they are the ones who classically complain about such things. But instead of answers, I get a pained, melancholic silence. One guy just gives me a hollow look and turns away.

No one wants to talk about sex, but they all will talk about shit. Endlessly. The shit that came out both ends at once, the shit that came out the neck of the babygro, the hard round shit and the shit that is soft and green. There is nothing new parents don't know about this substance. It makes me wonder why human beings bother with disgust, and whether we will ever be disgusted again.

On Christmas Day, the baby likes the wrapping paper, like every baby who has been in this house, and sat on this carpet and thrown the presents over their shoulder to eat the big, loud,

crinkly pictures. Such glorious repetition. Her besotted grandmother, her uncles, cousins and aunts. And I think there is a
deal of grief in all this – the family renewing itself in hope,
time after time.

The Seventh Month

Development (the baby)
The baby's eyes change colour. They are blue, edged with navy,
they are green with a smoky blue ring and, one day, amber
spreads through the iris. Is this you? Are these your final eyes?

I lift the baby over the threshold and carry her around the new
house. She loves the way one room unfolds into another, and
greets each space with delight. She leans forward, greedy for
the fact that corners exist and there is always something else
around them. She sits on the floor and likes the echo, and
shouts.

Regression (me)
I cannot remember this month. We have bought a house and
we are selling our flat. Or we haven't. There is a lot of talk
about bridging finance. Martin sits up late, night after night,
doing sums on scraps of paper. I cry a fair amount. Or stop
myself from crying.

I won't spend a night in the new house. It is cold, I say. It
is too far away. There is nowhere for the baby to sleep. I am
obsessed with her sleep. She will sleep in the car on the way
out to the house, but then we must leave the house, so she
can sleep on the way home.

Every day I bump the buggy down four flights of stairs to let people view the flat, then pull it back up four flights with the shopping hung off the handles. I look around the flat and I think that we are selling her entire world.

Meanwhile, I have to earn some money, and the baby won't sleep. When Martin walks in, I hand her over, or even push her towards him, and go to the computer, and will not be spoken to. He must be home in the evening. I must be home in the evening. We are both frozen. No one moves.

It is all too much.

The Eighth Month

Development (the baby)
The baby is in flying form, lying on her back and just laughing and kicking for no reason. I don't know what she is laughing at. Is this a memory? Is she imagining, for the first time, tickles, even though there are no tickles there?

She may be the only truly happy person on the planet. I look at her and hope she isn't bonkers.

Regression (me)
I close the door on the flat, busy with removals men. I don't say goodbye.

On the way to the new house, the clutch cable snaps in the fast lane of the dual carriageway as I gear down to stop at some traffic lights. I break the lights and crawl across the road to find the kerb in a slow swerve. I ring Martin, whose mobile is on answering machine. I ring my mother and father. I run down to a local pub with the baby in my arms and ask does anyone know a local garage. That fella over there owns one, they say. I get to the garage in first gear. And so on, and so forth.

Behind me, the removals men have left the washing–machine connection leaking into the flat, a fact we do not hear about until two days later, when the water spills into the hall. We still have no car. Martin stays late after work in order to dry out the flat while I unpack cardboard boxes – or try to, while looking after the baby – and complain, complain, complain. I have no time to work, I say. I don't even have time to unpack. How does it always, always, fucking end up like this, with the woman climbing a domestic Everest while the man walks out the door? I would go out and look for a nursery, but I have to start earning before I can pay for a nursery. I have to start earning to pay for the house.

There is a freak snowstorm. We have no milk. I put the baby in the buggy and, slithering along the path, I push her through the gale.

The Ninth Month

Development (the baby)
Spring. The child looks out into the garden at the changing light. There is something about this scene that she understands and I don't know what it is. I don't know if it is the tree – the fact that the tree is there, or that it is green, or that it is made of so many leaves. I do not know if it is the wind she likes, the way the tree moves when it blows. She raises her hand and starts to shout. It is a long, complicated shout, 'Aah aaah bleeh oh. Ahh nyha mang bwah!' She is making a speech. Her hand is lifted high; the palm reaches towards the sky as

she declaims. As far as I can tell there is nothing she wants in the garden, she just wants to say that it is there, and that it is good. She wants to say this loudly and at length.

The baba bears witness. The baba testifies.

Regression (me)

I have no notes for this month.

I unpack boxes. I hold the baby and love her, like a tragic event. She loves me like the best joke out.

On the day she is nine months old, I think that she has been outside of me, now, for just as long as she was inside. She is twice as old.

I am the mirror and the hinge. There she is. She is just as old as herself.

Time

My earliest memory is of a pot stand. It is set into a corner
with a cupboard on one side and, on the other, a shallow step.
This is where my head begins. The step leads to another room,
and far on the other side of the room, there is a white-haired
woman sitting in a chair.

Discussions with my mother lead to just one pot stand, in
a seaside cottage the summer I was eighteen months old. It
was, she says, made of black iron and it stood beside a real step
and the white-haired woman must be her own mother who
died when I was six. This image of her is all that I have, and
even then it is not so much an image as a sense. She may have
been asleep, but I think she was reading. And there was something very quiet and covert about the pot stand, which was a
pyramid affair with shelves for four pots. I can remember a
little saucepan on the top shelf. I am tempted to say that there
was a big saucepan on the bottom one, but this is pushing
things a bit. I would give anything to remember what the lino
was like.

At nine months, the baby puts her head in a pot and says,
Aaah Aaah Aaah. She says it very gently and listens to the echo.
She has discovered this all by herself. By way of celebration, I

put my own head into the pot and say, Aaah Aaah Aaah. Then she does it again. Then I do it again. And so on.

The rest of my family don't believe that I remember the pot stand, on the grounds that it is a stupid memory and, anyway, I was far too young. It is the job of families to reject each other's memories, even the pleasant ones, and being the youngest I am sometimes forced to fight for the contents of my own head. But my brother broke his elbow that summer. My mother had to take him to hospital in Dublin and my grandmother looked after us while she was away. This was the first time in my life that I was without my mother for any length of time. If she had stayed, then I am certain that I would not have remembered anything at all of that house – not the pot stand, and not my grandmother either.

We pilfer our own memories, we steal them from the world and salt them away.

I first left the baby when she was four months old. Some of the days when I was away, she spent with my mother. I wonder what image might remain with her from that time: a colour, a smell, a combination of shapes perhaps, affectless and still – and in the distance, someone. Just that. Someone.

And in the foreground? The carpet perhaps. I hope she remembers my parents' carpet, the one I remember as a child, with a pattern of green leaves like stepping-stones all the way down the hall.

I have another, possibly earlier, memory of pulling the wall-paper off the wall from between the bars of my cot. My mother is absent from this scene too, but though the Pot Stand Memory is neither happy nor unhappy, this one is quite thrilling. I almost certainly ate the paper. The plaster underneath it was pink and powdery, and I imagine now that I can remember the shivery taste of it. I also remember the shape of the tear on the wall, or I think I do. At any rate, I see it in my mind's eye – a seam on the left, stunningly straight, with four gammy strips pulled away, like a fat raggedy set of fingers, on the right.

I know this memory is, in some sense, true, but when I try to chase it, it disappears. It exists in peripheral vision, and presents itself only when I focus on something else – like typing, for example. When I stop writing this sentence and look up from the screen to try to see the pattern of the wallpaper – a blank. Memories, by their nature, may not be examined, and the mind's eye is not the eye we use, for example, to cross the road.

I wonder if this is the way that the baby sees things: vaguely and all at once. I imagine it to be a very emotional way to exist in the world. Perhaps I am being romantic – but the visual world yields nothing but delight to her. There are (it seems) no horrors, no frights. Tiny babies see only in monochrome. I imagine colour leaking into her head like a slowly adjusted screen – tremendously slow, like a vegetable television growing silently in the corner of the room. I imagine her focus becoming sharper and deeper, like some infinitely stoned cameraman adjusting his lens. 'Oh,' she says – or something that is the precursor to 'Oh', a shallow inhalation, a stillness as she is caught by something, and begins to stalk it: careful, rapt – the most beautiful sound in the world: the sound of a baby's wondering breath.

Something pulls in me when she is caught like this. For months I am a slave to her attention. The world is all colour, light and texture and I am her proud companion. I have no choice. None of us do. In a café, three women look over to smile at her, and then, as one, they look up. 'Oh, she likes the light,' says one, and this fact pleases us all. Immensely.

The light, of course, is horrible, and this is one of the reasons mothers think they are losing their minds: this pride in the baby looking at the light, this pride in the light as they introduce it to the baby, 'Yes, the light!' There is a certain zen to it; the world simple and new as we all stop to admire the baby admiring a wrought-iron candelabra with peculiar dangly bits and five – yes, five! – glowing, tulip-shaped bulbs.

She is years away from knowing from what 'five' might be, but maybe she already gets the 'fiveness' of it. This is the way her eyes move: One, one more! Another one! All of them! The other two. The first one again, another one! Something else.

Sometimes she holds her hand up like the baby Christ, and looks as though she contains everything, and understands it all. I do not ask to be forgiven, but still I feel redemption in the completeness of her gaze. And I feel the redemption in her fat baby wrists and her infinitely fine, fat baby's hand. The baby is a blessing, but sometimes she does, she *must,* also bless, which is to say that she simply sees, and lifts her hand, as a sign.

I pick the baby up and we look in the wardrobe mirror, which has always been for her a complicated delight: What is it? It's a baby! She smiles, it smiles back! (Complication upon complication! It's me! It's me! she says, and all her synapses, as I imagine, going ping! ping! ping!) She sees me smiling at her in the mirror; she sees her mother turning to smile at her in the room, and oh, it's too much, she lunges forwards to examine the knob on the wardrobe door.

There are actually two knobs on the wardrobe. One is wooden and the other, for some reason, is an amber-coloured plastic. The baby goes from one to the other and back again. One of the first confusions in her young life was when myself and Martin both looked at her at the same time: 'Oh no, there's two of them.' It almost felt unfair.

68

As she grew older, there was nothing she liked more than to be held by one of us and to look at the other, in a somewhat haughty way. Older still, she is completely content when the two of us are with her, quietly in a room. She has travelled from one, to two, perhaps to many. I think of this as she goes from the wooden knob to the amber one – a fairy tale of sameness and difference. This one. That one.

Of course, the first difference between this and the other is not between mother and father, or even between baby and 'baby in the mirror', but between one breast and . . . the other! If women had five teats, then mankind might, by now, be living on the moon.

Yesterday, it was warm, and I took off her socks and stood her on the grass. She loved this, but maybe not so much as I did – her first experience of grass. For her, this green stuff was just as different and as delicious as everything else – the 'first' was all mine. Sometimes, I feel as though I am introducing her to my own nostalgia for the world.

In the meantime, grass is green and springy and amazingly multiple and just itself. It might even be edible. Everything goes into her mouth. This is the taste of yellow. This is the taste of blue. Since she started moving about she has also experienced the taste of turf, of yesterday's toast, and probably of mouse droppings, because it was weeks before I realised we were not alone in the house. Paper remains her ultimate goal, and she looks over her shoulder now to check if I am around. That wallpaper looks nice.

I really do wish I could remember my own wallpaper, instead of just the tear I made in it. The baby sleeps in my cot now – the one my father made over forty years ago with some half-inch dowel, and a fairly ingenious sliding mechanism for the side to be let down. I sat beside it one night, feeding her, and I tried to remember what it was like to be inside; the view between the bars and the ripped wallpaper on the wall. Someone, over the years, had painted it nursery blue, but I remembered a green colour, I could almost recall chewing the cross bar at the top. The baby sucked, her eyelashes batting slowly over a drunken, surrendered gaze, and as my attention wandered I saw, under a chip in the blue paint, the very green I ate as a child. A strong and distant emotion washed briefly over me and was gone.

My mother, or someone, pulled the cot away from the wall and, in time, the wallpaper I do not remember was replaced with wallpaper that I do remember (flowers of blue, block-printed on white). Babies love pattern so much I have begun to regret my own attempts at tastefulness. Not a single curlicued carpet for her to crawl over, not a single flower on the wall. Even her toys are in primary colours and her mobile is from the Tate, cut-out shapes, like a Mondrian floating free.

Once I stop trying, I seem to remember my mother giving out to me about the ripped-up wall. She would have been upset about the wallpaper. Perhaps this is why I remember it. It was my first real experience of 'NO!'

My own child thinks No! is a game. I say it once and she pauses. I say it twice and she looks at me. I say it three times and she laughs. The punch-line!

Tasteful as it is, she loves the mobile. It has a big red circle that spins slowly to blue, and a little square that goes from black to white. There are various rectangles that don't particularly obsess her but, taken all in all, it is the thing she likes most in the world.

We moved when she was nearly eight months old, and it was another two weeks before I got round to stringing up the mobile for her again. When it was done, she shuddered with delight. It happened to her all in spasm. She realised, not only that the mobile was there, but also that it had once been gone. She remembered it. In order to do this she needed to see three things: the mobile in the old flat, the new room without the mobile, the new room with the mobile. Memory is not a single thing.

Martin says that his first memory, which is of one brother breaking a blue plastic jug over another brother's head, is false. His mother tells him that they never did have a slender, pale blue plastic jug. He thinks he dreamt about the jug, and that the dream also contained the idea that this was his first memory, as he dreamt a subsequent 'first memory' of people waving to him from a plane while he stood in the garden below. He was convinced for years that this was real. This makes me think that we are very young when we search for our first memory – that single moment when we entered the stream of time.

My own mother, who is curator and container of many things, among them the memory of my pot stand, worries that she is getting forgetful. The distant past is closer all the time, she says. If this is true, then the memory of her own mother is getting stronger now; sitting in a house by the sea, surrounded by children who are variously delighted, or worried, or concentrating on other things.

When you think about it, the pots can't have stayed there for long. I would have pulled them down. There would have been noise, though my memory of them is notably, and utterly, silent. Perhaps what I remember is the calm before a chaos of sound and recrimination. That delicious, slow moment, when a baby goes very, very quiet, knowing it is about to be found out.

The other morning, the baby (silently) reached the seedlings I have under the window, and she filled her mouth with a handful of hardy annuals and potting compost. I tried to prise her mouth open to get the stuff out. She clamped it shut. She bit me (by accident). She started to cry. When she cried, her mouth opened. She was undone by her own distress and this seemed so unfair to me that I left her to it. I hadn't the heart. Besides, it said on the pack that the compost was sterilised.

But she will not let my finger into her mouth, now, even to check for a tooth (she is very proud of her teeth), and when she clamps it shut and turns away she is saying, 'Me,' loud and clear. 'Oh,' a friend said, when she started to crawl, 'it's the beginning of the end,' and I knew what she meant. It is the beginning of the end of a romance between a woman who has forgotten who she is and a child who does not yet know.

Until one day there will come a moment, delightful or banal, ordinary or strange, that she will remember for the rest of her life.

Advice

It is the middle of the morning – an ordinary morning of undressing, dressing, sterilising, mixing, spooning, wiping, squawking, smiling, banging, reaching for the bread knife, falling down, climbing up, in the middle of which – a crisis! which is dealt with in the military style: change nappy, remove shitty vest, wash hands, find clean vest, pull baby away from stairs, comfort baby when she cries for stairs, dress baby, lift shitty vest, soak shitty vest, wash hands, and finally we are out the door and into the car seat, off to the supermarket, me singing 'Twinkle Twinkle Little Star' and remembering I have left the back door wide open. I am driving carefully. The sun is shining. I think, What will I tell her when she grows up? Actually I think, What if I die? What if I die, now, soon, or even later on? I am in the throes of car accidents and chemotherapy, between the first twinkle twinkle and the second twinkle twinkle. By the fourth repetition, she is trying to dress herself for school and wandering out of the house alone. Her father has disappeared from this fantasy. She is facing the wide world, and there is nothing I can do to help her. I cannot reach her, I cannot speak. I should write her a letter, but what could it say?

Park, take the baby out of car seat, try to find keys, put the baby back in car seat, find keys, take the baby out of car seat, lock car, and so on, all the way through the coin for the trolley (leave baby down on the ground? Is that dog shit? Who would have thought there could be so much shit in the world?), I am banishing foolish thoughts. They are just the big metaphysics, swooping over our small, lovely life. I must try to live in the middle, think in a middling way, and so, as we sail along the aisles, as I keep hold of her arm while ducking down, over and over again, to pick up the half-chewed, as yet unpaid-for banana that she enjoys throwing out of the trolley, I concentrate on a simpler task. Advice. What advice can you give a child to arm and protect them in the world? I am not thinking of *Don't talk to strangers*, but of the things that only I would say. This is the perk that every mother demands, somewhere along the line – to exercise her own, particular personality. Usually, let's admit it, with disastrous results.

Smile at the checkout, apologise for the banana, sing, 'Do You Love an Apple,' to keep her still in the paused trolley, search busily through my empty head, only one nugget comes to mind. *Beware of modest people. They are the worst megalomaniacs of all.*

For the rest of the day (scrub out the shitty vest? No, throw out the shitty vest. Don't tell anyone), this is the only wisdom I can find, the only sentence, *Beware of modest people* . . . of course it is true: Einstein, Mother Teresa, some women I know, many many nuns, a couple of poets – all so lovely, all so monstrous. You have to have a very big ego to wrestle it down to something so small. I know, I've tried. *Beware the tender smile, my daughter, the love that saddens, the crinkly eyes* . . .

But it isn't exactly useful, as advice goes. Not as useful as

Don't touch the oven, it is hot! which is what I spend my day saying, now. *Hot! Hot!* I would also say, *Dirty! Dirty!* but I can't be bothered. I concentrate on *Careful!* or *Gently!* or plain *NO!* And so it will be, for years yet. The first thousand days of her life, the whole remarkable world around her, and all that I have to say could be reduced to one phrase, *Proceed . . . with caution.* And for the thousand days after that? *Don't talk to strangers,* of course, which is the same thing again, in a way.

There must be more. I just can't think of anything. I open my mouth and . . . my own mother comes falling out of it. But of course.

She takes advice very seriously, my mother. She still doles it out on a regular basis. She is not afraid to repeat herself. She is often right – when, for example, she says to me, *You should flatter people a little. You should at least try.*

I never listened to a word of it; except maybe for, *If Joyce was worried about what his Mammy might say, he would never have written* Ulysses (a piece of advice which she has paid for, many times since), or the excellent, *Never use a big word where a small word will do.* What about, *Cheer up, we'll soon be dead*? Did she really say that? Of course she would deny it, now – though I still find it giddily bleak and quite useful. *Cheer up, we'll soon be dead,* just one of her variations on the mother's mantra of, *All this will pass.* Having the wrong pencil-case, being forced to share a desk with Brenda Dunne, losing the boy you love, *In fifty years' time you might even laugh about it* (but what happens, Ma, when you run out of time?)

Never laugh at someone's religion, that's a good one. Actually, what she said was, 'If someone worships a stone in the road and you laugh at them, they will pick it up and hit you with it.' Fair enough.

75

I didn't start arguing with her until it came to men. *Never humiliate a man in public* – intriguing, this one. What were you to do in private? And then again, some men are very easily humiliated. They are humiliated when you are clever, and it is hard work being stupid. They are humiliated if you flirt, or if you don't flirt. You could spend your life tending to some man's pride, but, *There is no excuse for marrying a bastard*, she said, or something like it, as if falling for the wrong man was just a lazy way to go about your life, when there were so many good men in the world. In those days, a Good Man was someone who allowed the household the use of his pay-packet, who wasn't a drunk, and who didn't hit you. Actually, this is probably still a good baseline. Maybe this is something I could pass on to my daughter. I could translate it as:

Never sleep with someone who has more problems than you – 50 per cent of people fail to follow this advice, and it is vital to be in the other half. What else?

Never trust someone beyond their strength, because – oh, my darling girl, and the million things that could hurt her; not strangers, but friends, because these are the ones who break your heart – she must arm herself against the weak more than the strong . . .

'Oh, get a grip, Mother.'

All advice is useless. *Don't wear patterns next to your face. Never plant camellias facing east. Have sex before you go out for the night, not after you come home. The things that make you fat are booze and biscuits – nothing else.* What about, *Earn money* – my mother used to tell me to do this all the time. All right. *Earn money* – you must overcome the natural distaste you might feel for cash. If you dislike the system, then find a crack in it, and live there. And the simplest way to earn money is to go out and earn it. That is what is called the (middle–class) Tao of money.

I didn't listen to that either.

And look at this baby, just look at her – with her steady baby's gaze; her serious baby's eyes that have some joke in them all the same, as she putters towards the plastic shopping bags.

'No!' I shout, and when she cries I say, 'It's all right. It's all right.'

Proceed with caution.

Actually, most of the time I don't know what 'No' is for. Mind the door, mind the books don't fall, mind your fingers, hot!, careful of the cup, don't touch the dirt. After one particularly long day, I decided against it. It was making me depressed. So I left her to her own devices for a while, and we all cheered up.

The Sioux, Martin tells me, let their babies learn everything for themselves: fall into the river, fall into the fire, anything. But children are quite careful, really.

And what does she say to me?

'Burr!' says the baby, pointing at the sky.

Look at the bird, Mama. This is my baby's advice to me. *Look at the bird!*

Being Two

'**I**'m two,' she says, standing on the bathroom scales. And indeed there it is on the dial, the nice, round-topped, swoop and swan of '2'. She is fond of being two. She is nearly three. Her new little brother is only zero with a few silly bits added on. He is not even a proper number yet.

'So how's it all going?'

I want to tell people about her, but I want to tell them *everything* about her, because there is nothing else. The proper maternal mode is gabble. The proper maternal instrument is the phone. We are all a Jewish joke.

'She can read! She read her name on her birthday card!'

'And what about the number?'

'No problem. Twenty-one.'

And I want to tell them nothing about her. She is a child, she must not be described. She must be kept fluid and open; not labelled or marked. I could say that she is playful, open, stubborn, bossy, winsome, serious, giddy, boisterous, clinging, gorgeous – but these are words that describe every single two-year-old on the planet, they are not the essence of herself, the thing that will always be there. Describing a child is a matter of prediction or nostalgia. There is no present moment. You are always trying to grasp something that changes even as you look at it. Besides, all children are the same, somehow. And still I know she is different from the general run of toddlers. How do I know? I just do. And if you think I am biased, this is what other people have said about her:

'There's no doubt about it, she is a fabulous child.'

Donal Enright, Grandfather.

'I have to say I never met a more interesting, or nicer, two-year-old.'

Theo Dombrowski, a friend.

'She is very advanced for two, and I should know – I am an educational psychologist.'

Stranger (possibly mad), in the foyer of a West Cork hotel.

'Oh, all her geese are swans,' my mother used to say about boastful mothers.

In the old days – as we call the 1970s, in Ireland – a mother would disparaise her child automatically. I understand this urge: you don't want a toddler to get the edge on you, especially when you are trying to get them past a shop full of sweets; so 'She's a monkey,' a mother might say, or 'Street angel, home devil,' or even my favourite, 'She'll have me in an early grave.'

It was all part of growing up in a country where praise of any sort was taboo. Of course we are nicer now, we are more confident and positive and relaxed – which does not explain the strange urge I had when a man looked at her photograph. 'Such lovely eyes,' he said, and I said, 'Oh, they're all right,' or something even worse. It is true that I felt acutely, burningly praised, but I also felt the deep hiss of a mother who reaches out her hand to say, *Give me back my baby.*

People don't write much about their children. Sometimes they say it is to protect the child's privacy – but I am not sure how private a ten-year-old feels, for example, about a picture of his two-year-old self, or how connected. I think it is simpler than that. I think people don't want to write about their children because they think that, if they do, their children might die. And that's just for starters. I think they do not want to surrender any part of their children, certainly not for money, and particularly not to a crowd.

So this is just a mock-up. It is not the real girl at all.

'You have a smelly bum.'

'Go away. Go smell your own bum.'

'I can't smell my bum. I can't get my face around.'

She already loves a paradox, and most of them are anatomical. 'A shark has a long nose so he can't see his mouth,' she says (well, you know what she means). Which reminds me, I must get her *Alice in Wonderland*, though:

'That's me,' she said, a while ago.

'Where?'

'In that car.'

'Oh. You're in that car?'

'Yes.'

'Where are you going?'

'I going to my house.'

'Where is your house? What kind of house?'

'It has a yellow door.'

'Oh.'

After a while, I say, 'And what is your name?'

'Alice,' she says.

This spooked me no end. She is not called Alice, and we

do not have a yellow (or lello) door. I thought she was having a past-life regression, there in the back of the car – well, I didn't really, but sometimes I wish I was that bit more credulous. Then later, in the bath, she was all talk of rabbits and my-ears-and-whiskers, and I realised that she had heard, or seen, her first ever *Alice in Wonderland*.

Fantastic. The rabbit went down the plug hole, in the end.

Her father must have been away if I was giving her a bath – these more intriguing dialogues happen when her ordinary life is unbalanced in some way.

'I love him,' she says, pointing at the picture of the author on the back of one of her books. Colin McNaughton, he is called – a very pleasant, handsome-looking guy. I have to admire her taste, though the writer thing is a bit unsettling. Never fall for a writer, I want to say. Never, ever, ever make that mistake.

Instead I say, 'Oh.'

'Yes. Because my Dada is away.'

This is nothing (I flatter myself) to the anxiety she feels when her mother is away. Endlessly recounted is the story of the witch in the supermarket, last Hallowe'en. A woman in a mask who came up and, I presume, cackled at her while she was sitting in the trolley and then, when the child started to cry, took off the witch's mask to show that she was only a nice person underneath. Silly bitch. I think taking the mask off made it worse, but there you go; I suppose it's too late to sue. Later that evening, she stood with her father in the dark, watching the local fireworks from an upstairs window. When I came home, there were spent rockets in the flower-beds.

A hundred renditions of the witch-in-the-supermarket story later, I hit on the key. I was away at the time – does she remember? She certainly does. She remembers that I was in Paris. What was I doing in there? she suddenly asks, Was I frightened? Was I watching the fireworks, too?

'I was,' I say, and once I am placed in the picture – somewhere on the other side of the fireworks – the story is allowed to fade. But she is still obsessed by witches, which is presumably, somehow, my fault – also bad fairies and wicked stepmothers. There are no nice women in the old stories. Though one morning she announces a dream – a good dream. What was it about?

'Barbie,' she says, looking very coy.

'Oh? And what was Barbie doing?'

'She was reading me a book.'

Which is one of the things that I do, of course – my tendency to interpret the child mocked by an image of myself as a six-foot plastic toy. And maybe it is not all a drama of good mother / bad mother, maybe she was just angling for a Barbie and knows how much I'd love to know what happens in her dreams. She is two. She has – perhaps they all have – a delicious mind.

She has a quality, sometimes, when she is tired. Her eyes become distant, and slightly blissed. She looks at you strangely, as though she has been here before.

I am heavily pregnant and under the shower. We are alone in the house, and I think, What would happen if I fell? Would she be able to fetch the phone? I can see it all: the gravid woman, wedged into the bath, the water playing on her senseless belly, the toddler bereft, the time passing; all this flashing through my mind in a moment, while she tilts her face up to me, and says, 'Don't fall.'

Or I am going up the stairs with her in my arms. I think, I must ring my mother and she says, 'Does Granny have stairs?'

They are so tiny and inconsequential, these coincidences of mind. They always surprise me, even though they are not so surprising – after all, for most of the time we live the same life – and I begin to build a little wall against my Midwich Cuckoo. Some of my thoughts are so unbecoming. I catch myself and think, 'I hope she didn't get that one.'

All of this is very slight, you understand, and nothing you could absolutely put a finger on. It never involves a future event, but when she talks about someone, I might ring them, just to check that they are still alive. They always are.

I tell her about her Granny and Granda, how they met at a dance, in a hotel by the sea. She says, 'Was I watching?'

I am tempted to say, 'I don't know.'

What else?

She is very bossy about the world. She is always putting it in its place and sometimes there is very little difference between ordering it, and ordering it around. 'Cars don't go into houses, they are too big.' 'That car [a convertible] has no lid.' 'Cars have roofs and motor bikes have helmets.'

Yes,' I say to all this. I have to say, Yes, or she will repeat it ad infinitum. 'Yes. Yes, absolutely. Yes.'

For months we were trapped in a kind of Beckettian rhapsody, as she tried to make the world safe. From the back seat:

'Mama, cars don't go into houses, do they?'

'No, they don't.'

'Do they?'

'No, they certainly don't, they're too big.'

'And they don't go on the path.'

'No.'

'They go on the road.'

'Yes.'

'People go on the path.'

'Yes. Absolutely.'

'Where's it gone?'

'Where's what gone?'

'Where's the street light gone?'

'It's behind us.'

'But where's it gone?'

'We'll see another one.'

'But where's it gone?'

'Oh, take it easy.'

It happens on the same stretch of road – she always grieves the disappearing street lights: the way they keep coming, only to flick away.

It was around here that I once said, 'I used to work over there, before you were born.'

'When I was a baby.'

'No, before that. Before you were born.'

'When I was just a teeny-tiny baby?'

'No, before you were even here. Before you were in my tummy.'

'I was . . . Where.'

'You were just a twinkle in your Daddy's eye.'

'I not a twinkle. I NOT a twinkle!!!' And she started to kick and squawk. I suppose I did sound a little smug; a little complacent about the idea that she was once non-existent. Too tough, really, for any age, but especially tough for two.

Her favourite story is *Sleeping Beauty*. But only recently. Fairy tales happened in the last few weeks, at the end of 'two' and the beginning of 'nearly three', because 'two' is a very long place. She started the year obsessed by gender, moved into a long toilet phase, and ended with witches, princesses, and sleep.

But also in there were numbers, which gave her huge pleasure, as did all kinds of repetition and ritual and make-believe. There was also the endless amusement to be got from ordering her parents around and giving them grief.

'Not the blue cup with the straw.'

'I thought you wanted a straw.'

'I don't want a straw.'

'Do you want the blue cup?'

'I don't want a straw.'

'OK.'

'I don't want a straw!'

And so on, all the way to wails, screams, tears. Of course the dialogue is edited to make me look like a saint, which I am not. ('The cup goes in the bin. All right? The cup – see this cup? – it's going in the bin.') Months of attrition later I realise that the best thing to do is to become benignly invisible. If I can manage simply not to exist, there is no escalation.

She is only two.

Though sometimes, I am two, too.

And when she has done every single, possible thing to provoke, thwart, whine, refuse, baulk, delay, complicate and annoy, I wonder how the human race survived.

'I'll swing for you,' I heard myself saying once. Which is Irish for 'I will kill you and take the consequences.'

She is two. She is *only* two.

There is nothing better than watching her play shopping. When she walks across the room to the 'shops' she does not so much walk as 'walk' with an exaggeration of hip and heel that says, 'Here I am "walking" to the shops.' She hums to the rhythm of it. Hum. Hum. Hum. Hum. Walk. Walk. Walk. Walk.

All her inverted commas are huge, and even in ordinary conversation she will sometimes use an 'other' voice; fake wise, or fake grown-up, with much use of the word 'actually'. As in, 'That looks like a duck, actually.'

There is a place on the wall where she gets things, like broccoli, or sweets, or water. She runs over to the wall and goes, 'Ssszzsst,' rolling and twiddling her hands in a 'complicated' way. Then she runs back from the wall with my imaginary cup of tea.

'Oh, *thank* you.'

Her anxiety about the baby that is on the way brings back all kinds of eating games. 'Gobble gobble nyum nyum,' she says, 'I am eating your arm.' She does not like it so much when I eat her back. 'Nyum nyum, scarf scarf gobble nyum.' She runs to her special place on the wall and takes down bits of herself, which she sticks along her arm, and pats back into place. She is getting her real arm back, she says. I have just eaten her pretend one.

'Yes,' I say, thinking, as I often do, that she is an outrageously wonderful child. Sometimes, of course, she is just outrageous.

She is two.

'Can I be two?' I say, and have a pretend tantrum on the floor. Just a small one. I lie on my back and drum my heels. She doesn't like the look of this at all.

It is a very long year. When November comes I miss the child October gave us, that paradise, when I was only moderately pregnant and potty training had not yet begun. And I miss the baby, just walking, who looked at the black and yellow stripes of the Kilkenny hurling team and said, 'Bees! Bees!'

This is the girl who was entranced by every flying thing, who followed a plane across the sky in her Granny's back garden and never took her eyes away once, whose first or second word may have been 'bird', whose first big word was 'helicopter', who can already tell a hoverfly from a bee (but not a bee from a wasp), and a tweet-tweet birdie from one that goes caw-caw. This is the girl who got 'a moth' from Santa Claus for Christmas. She is also, of course, fond of woodlice, but give her a glider, a kite, a cloud, a woman under a parachute, a fairy, or a balloon, and she will choose them over a slug or snail any day. She is close to the ground, which might be the reason that she is always looking up, but the reason she loves butterflies is the reason she likes the mirror and also the reason that she likes hands: it is that one side is the same as the other side, and nothing has given her greater joy, I think, than folding a piece of paper over some splashes of paint, and opening a Rorschach of complete delight. It is always a butterfly, because this is the best thing it could be, and other things that mirror and match are butterflies too.

'A bum is like a butterfly,' she said once.

'Yes. Yes.'

The first play she ever went to was about bees and, when the actors gave her a set of paper wings, she declared into the stillness of the audience, 'I can fly.'

Of Christ on the Cross she says, 'Are they wings?' and I say, 'No, darling, those are His arms.'

'When I was a little baby,' she says, wrestling with the idea of growing up, now that there is another baby in Mammy's tummy.

'When I was a little baby,' she says (because these things are always said twice), 'I used to say "pine-a-cacket".'

'And what do you say now?'

'I say, "pineapple".'

We are both amused by this. We are both fond of her former self. Now she is a big girl, she looks with tenderness at a picture of herself newborn. 'Look how pleased your Dada is to see you,' I say. She looks at this for a while, and then walks over to embrace him, properly and formally. Sometimes she has astonishing emotional clarity; and I have to catch my breath at the rightness of her.

She is nearly three. She is learning, she told me, not to cry at things. I said she could still cry at some things but she shook her head. No, she would not cry. And when she is three, she says, she will not be scared of the witch in the supermarket. It is a serious business, growing up; a heavy responsibility.

On the Friday before her birthday, I bring a (pink!) cake into the crèche, and she asks, 'I'm going to have a cake, even though I am still two?' and I realise that it is not the cake, or the candles, or the party, or the presents that matter to her, so much as *being three*. It is a different place.

Groundhog Day

When I was a child, I used to ask my mother about childbirth and how much it hurt and she would always say, 'You know, you forget.'

I thought she was being tactful. After all, I was the source of the pain – if you could call that emerging thing 'me'.

'But does it hurt, though? Does it?'

'Yes,' she might say, eventually. 'But really – you forget.'

Later I thought it was a Catholic thing, a long-suffering thing, an attempt to sucker me into the reproduction game. But there was an edge to her voice, or a distance. Was this fear, or outrage? Was it the sound of my mother lying?

'How could you forget?'

Now I know what it was. It was the push in someone's voice when they are trying to get at the actual, real truth of something: the central paradox, you might say. And I also know what that truth is:

You FORGET!!!

So there I am, lying half-assed on the fully adjustable birthing bed – quite literally, because the epidural is spreading, or not spreading, from one side of me to the other, so that one leg is all tingling and the other a dead weight. Lying there, as I say, with an enormous weight bearing out of one, but not the other, side of my backside, so that it feels as though I am giving birth in segments, and all I can think is, 'How did I forget? How COULD I forget this?! How could anyone?'

There is something quite dispiriting about a second birth — you feel like such a fool.

'Isn't nature wonderful?' my mother says. By which she means, Isn't God wonderfully clever to make us all as stupid as we are?

Of course, technically speaking, it isn't your arse that the weight is pushing into, or out of, it isn't your backside, so much as your frontside. So I should say 'vagina' or 'birth canal'. But really — a baby rearranges your body, it shoulders your kidneys out of the way, it flattens your bladder with its head, squishes your intestines like an intemperate cook squeezing the meat out of a string of sausages; a baby obliges your legs to pop out of their sockets, and it doesn't care whether they pop back in again once it is through — and where is all this happening? 'Vagina' is too small a word somehow — 'vagina' is just an indication of where its path might lie, 'vagina' is just a *direction*.

I prefer 'soft tissue'. A baby makes its way out of your body through the softest route available, and for quite a while on that fully adjustable birthing bed, I feel as though the softest route is a dead end.

I am being enjoined to push, and I do push. I push very hard. I keep pushing. And then I push again. And for some time — seconds, or minutes, or more — I feel that all this was not a good idea: I feel it as a drowning person might feel about the inclination to go for a swim. The consequences are too huge. I am flat against the thing itself again. I am looking at the thing itself *again*, and the violence of it, the implacability, shocks me just as it did the last time. I think, How could I forget this? How reduced you become. And sometimes that is just great and sometimes . . . Christ.

I do not think I can get this baby out.

This is how people used to die.

In the circumstances, there is something banal about the room. The door opens like an ordinary door. People come through it. First the student midwife, full of chat, then the midwife, fast and effective (it is in a hurry, this baby); she organises the epidural and then works on me, doing – I don't know what; it feels as if someone is taking a light bulb out of a too-narrow shade. After her, the sister in charge, easy and reassuring. Then the consultant, who stares a little fixedly at the business end. Waking up. It is 3.00 a.m. Who will come in next? The master of the hospital, the Minister for Health, and then perhaps, God, as the baby puts its head out to taste the air.

They are looking after me. And like the prayer for those in peril on the sea, I feel there should be a hymn at least for the night workers who toil through the storm of childbirth, pushing, hauling, shouting, while the rest of the world sleeps.

'Push!'

I can't see down. I am sure that there is something they are not telling me and I am cold, all the way through. I don't remember being cold. Was it like this before? Was it worse? This baby is bigger, perhaps. I remember all this, as it happens; and it is all completely new.

The body has no imagination; this is why you never take a jumper with you on a warm day, just in case. The body has no memory, which is why sex is always such a surprise. The body lives in the present tense. The body makes a fool of you, every time.

'Push!'

They put me on my side for a while to save my pelvis, but that doesn't work, so they put me on my back again, but still I feel sort of crocked and wrong – like insomnia, but magnified. I feel like that picture in *Alice in Wonderland* where she has grown to fill the house – I can't get a purchase, somehow, on myself, and the baby, it seems to me, is heading in the wrong direction entirely.

They are trying to take it easy with my pelvis because, over the last while, it has become apparent that the last birth left it all a bit . . . disjointed. As the ligaments softened with this second pregnancy, the bones started to ease away from each other, like a slowly cracking bowl. Somewhere in the fifth month, I sat down on the floor of the hall to untie my daughter's shoe, and realised that I could not get up again. Also, that I would have to stay like this until her father came home, which might be in half an hour, or forty minutes – or maybe he had a meeting I had forgotten about, it could be any time at all. In fact, it was just twenty minutes, which we whiled away quite merrily, singing songs, for example, or 'having a little chat', until she ran up and down the hall taking off not just her shoes, but all her clothes, up to, and then including, her nappy which mercifully contained only pee. And this was all fine and really quite funny, except I couldn't walk.

The physiotherapist gave me some exercises which helped a lot, and I got a stretchy belt to support my pelvis which I was delighted to call a 'truss'; and the world separated, very cleanly, into those people who are nice to you when you are in pain, and those who are not. The ways in which they are not, and the reasons why they are not, is a vastly interesting subject, but I had no time to think about it, because I was in pain. I was fine sitting in a chair but in order to walk, or climb the stairs, I had to tune people out so that they became distant and slightly distorted. Pain is a muted, and empty, and mildly paranoid place. Which is to say that you would be paranoid if you had the space for it – in the meantime, you get by on a little irritation.

The body is an optimist: it always tells you the pain is waning, the pain is nearly gone. At this rate, you always think, it will be fine by morning. So I was always nearly better, and there was no point making a fuss. I sat down for most of the time, and promised myself that, once this was done, I would never turn down a paracetamol again.

But it is hard to control a two-year-old without getting up out of your chair. One morning when her father is away, and I have lost my stretchy belt, and I cannot blandish, cajole, or threaten this toddler into her clothes in order to bring her down to the crèche, I go downstairs and weep loud, salt tears. I weep for twenty minutes or so and go back up to a shocked, and slightly hilarious, little girl and we 'start again', and it doesn't work this time either. So I go and weep some more, and because this isn't good for her, and I can see no end to it, I climb the stairs again and announce a change of plan. We pack a bag and get into the car and drive to my parents' house, where there is – as you must know – a video of the *Teletubbies*, and we ring at the door. My mother is in her seventies, so she probably had mixed feelings when she found her middle-aged, half-mad, pregnant daughter on the doorstep, with a wired, gorgeous grandchild in tow. But she took us in, and I slept for three days.

All this by way of explaining why I was put on my side on the birthing bed. The midwives are totally clued in – they ask do I have a belt, or a frame – by which, I realise with a shock, they mean 'Zimmer frame'. One says that the latest medical study claims that pelvic problems like mine don't exist. Later, another says, 'We send them out of here on crutches all the time.' So why have I never heard of this before? It seems that, even now, there is a distance between what women say about themselves (I am in pain), and the degree to which this is seen as relevant (Ah, yes. Pain). But why should I be annoyed, when the one who denies it most is me?

Suffer on.

Oh, all right then.

The body forgets. The pains of this pregnancy, like the pains of the last, will wash through me like water. What I will always remember, though, what I can't forget, is the way people seemed to enjoy it – my joyful suffering – some of them in a kind way, and some in a way that was quite vicious. In the old days, it was women – the mad midwife who says to a labouring woman, 'Now you're paying for your five minutes of pleasure, cackle, cackle.' Or the mad matron who wouldn't let a friend take a cushion into the hospital church after the birth of her son. All the demented Catholic bitches fretting at their crochet blankets in the old people's homes, shouting, 'It serves you right!' and 'Filth! filth!' at the Latvian girl who comes in to hoover the floor. But the people who enjoyed my pain, in 2003, were men – very few, it has to be said, but it only takes one to ruin your day. The occasional drunken rant or sober sneering to tell me that I was weak, now. To remind me that, pregnant, I was a woman in the abstract, a slow-motion explosion of flesh and sexual anxiety, God help me, when all I was doing was trying to walk from one side of the room to the other.

94

The statistic you hear bandied about is that one in six women is abused during pregnancy. I assume this means 'hit'.

They are trying to call us back to the world, perhaps. They forget, as the pregnant woman forgets, that all this will end. Pregnancy is something that passes through your body. It is not about you, or even about itself. It is just a baby; endlessly, slowly, painfully, making its way out into the world.

The baby. The baby. Because of all this pelvis nonsense, I haven't had *time* to fall in love with the baby. And there is something in me now that is afraid of my own bones, that whispers, 'You will never walk again.' Maybe this is why the pushing doesn't go so well.

'Push!'

Everything looks like a home video in which some shots are endless, for no reason at all, and then it jumps to something else.

'Push!'

I pop a few blood vessels, apparently. Tiny ones, under my chin.

'Push.'

I do what they tell me. And then I don't want to do it any more. It is not a question of the pain. I don't think I am in pain – or at least, I am not sure. The room is quite ordinary, the people quite usual and nice, but I know something now that I never wanted to know. I know that the body is tough, and difficult, and that it can be broken. I know that when it is broken there is nothing left of you. This isn't so much a knowledge as a place and, afterwards, I do not want to go there again. If I do, I will recognise it, and know I am about to die, in the ordinary way that people do. What a sickener. Martin looks down at me – just a glance. And we go on.

'But did it hurt, though, Mam? Did it?'

'Ah,' says my mother, who did all of this in the days before epidurals. 'But wasn't it worth it?'

He is in the pram beside me now, sucking on his fingers, getting written about. Poor fella. His eyes have a gentle, mischievous look to them. 'It's nothing to do with me,' he says. Quite right. Two days ago, he discovered he could grasp things and he spent the rest of the day crying for the world: the pattern on the duvet that he could not pick up, his mother's hair that hung within reach and then was gone. He did not sleep for eleven hours – everything he saw, now, was something he might touch and hold. It's an exciting life.

It is exciting, having him around. The most surprising thing is the way that the love repeats as much as the pain – you would think there could not be enough space for it, and then, *creak,* another room opens in your heart, huge, full of interest and light. My beautiful boy. No, really – he came out handsome. I didn't see his first breath but I saw him when they held him up, a proper baby; grown up already, fat like a cherub and kicking against open air.

I have a baby the size of Marlon Brando.

'Hello.'

They lift him up high and already he looks so far away from me. A boy; I knew he would be a boy (I just did). I reach out and he is laid on my stomach, which sags terrifically to receive him. He does not stop crying, but he is not crying very hard. He takes his own time about things. He sorts himself out. I have the strongest feeling that he is his own person – a person I don't know yet, and may never actually know. This is the thrill of separation, and there is bleakness to it, too.

Someone new.

Then I lift him to my breast. How funny . . . I can't remember how to feed these things.

And the next night, when I still haven't got the hang of it, the night nurse whisks him off to produce an adult belch from somewhere (maybe she did it herself) and I think, 'Oh, Christ, *wind*. How could I forget about wind?' And some days later again, the same, stony-faced argument over the car seat – what origami do you do with the seat-belt, back or front, and facing which way? – as there was when his sister was born, and I stood on the side of the same road with a newborn baby in my arms.

And I know what the edge in my mother's voice was – it was wonder. An appalled sort of wonder. You forget. How can your mind let you down like that? How can you be such an amnesiac as to repeat the experience, as she did, *four more times*? The most important and intense moments of your life, the emotion-sodden weeks and months of nursing a new person into the world, wiped, gone; locked in some part of your mind to which you have no access. Where is it written – in your bones? Certainly not in the flesh, because flesh grows again, this is the mystery of it, everything springs back into (roughly) the right place; your bruised soft tissue plumps up again, and the cells that contain the secret of your last baby give way to cells that are indifferent and ready; perhaps even mildly disposed towards Doing It All Again.

When the baby is a month old – he is so gorgeous – I come, momentously, to a decision. I can't help it. I just have to say it. Of course I should bide my time, I should wait a month, or more: I should be canny about this thing, because this is an argument I feel I must win – but I end up blurting it out instead.

I say, 'I really think we should have another one. I really do.'

And Martin says, 'I am trying to drive the car.'

Science

I remember reading once that women have a thing in their brains, A Deep Thing, like a radar, that checks every forty-five seconds for the sound of a baby's cry. Whether you know it or not. Whether, even, you have a baby or not. And this, they say, is one of the reasons that women get up in the middle of the night to tend to crying babies.

So what's wrong with me?

I sleep. At least some nights I do. I sleep until the crying gets loud enough to wake me – as loud as the sound of a breaking cup, for example; slightly louder than the sound of the phone in another room (which doesn't wake me either). Martin gets up and brings the baby to me, and when Martin isn't there – well, there is no telling, really, how long that poor child might cry. I love my baby, but I am not a proper woman, neurologically speaking, or I have an override system, or the scientists who discovered the Deep Female Caring Thing in the Middle of Your Brain in the Middle of the Night were talking bollocks.

My life is littered with this stuff: a rubbish of studies and statistics about men, women, babies, cleaning fluids, neurologies, fatty acids, and what we are really like, and not one of them with a mental footnote to say where they came from – who studied what in order to decide them, and would you give them the time of day if they were sat beside you in the pub. They'll give people money to study anything these days: gender science, media science, why people in the Western world are mildly irritated with each other all the time now, why men earn more.

For example: there is a study that shows that men have a better grasp of three-dimensional space than women – and this is why they are better at reading maps. The scientists discovered this by scanning people's brains while they played certain computer games. Now, it may be that men are just better at computer games than women, or it may be that they have wasted more of their life playing computer games. Or it may, quite simply, be true. But what I want to know is, if men are so good at three-dimensional space, why can they never find anything around the house?

I'd love to have a brain scan. There's your head, like an electric cauliflower, all lit up in contours of red and orange and green. There is your brain all pulsing as you think of – well, who is to say *what* is going on in there. Don't tell the scientists, at any rate. Apparently, women's brains have a bigger – but *much* bigger – area for the emotion we call 'sad'. The scientists showed them 'sad things' and watched their brains flare. The report didn't say what the sad things were.

That is the problem with science. It never tells you the most important thing.

Here are some arbitrary facts. Men who do more about the house 'get' (as they say) more sex from their female partners. In homes where both partners are working full-time, women do the bulk of the housework, but the higher the status of the woman's job, the *more* work she does at home. (No sex there, so. Nice clean bathroom for you. Occasional holiday in the Caribbean. Fair enough.) People who look after children are more intelligent than people who do not (we knew that already). A child's impulse control depends on the amount of 'face time' it gets from its mother in the first eight months (read that and weep, girls). One-third of boys reared by single fathers in Britain end up in prison. Fifty-five per cent of Irish couples need both salaries to repay their mortgage. The number of Filipinas working as domestics in the southern suburbs of Dublin is a lot more than you think.

What single thing would most improve the quality of your life?

If my husband unballed his socks before they solidified in the laundry basket, that is the thing that would improve my life the most. If he afforded me and my labour that much respect.

Then again, he does the dishes. Even my porridge bowl. Even the scrambled eggs.

Every couple you meet is in an advanced stage of negotiation, whether they have children or not. You can spend weeks talking about who should be responsible for buying new light bulbs. You can spend your life talking about it, because when you talk about new light bulbs you are talking about everything. You are talking about how you were reared, and how you love, and how you are valued. Every light bulb is a triumph of diplomacy. It takes years to buy one. Marriage is like Churchill and Stalin breaking off, at Yalta, for a quick shag. Oh, all right then, you take Poland.

Meanwhile . . . I sit at my lovely desk, typing, while my lovely husband sits next door rocking my lovely baby with his foot and reading the newspaper. We are the most fortunate people that history has ever made. And I think that we will be devoured by plague and by fire, that the sea will rise up to drown us, and the bombs fall on us, and the food rot on our table. And still, clickety clickety click; rock, rock, rock. It is a lovely day, the sun pours through a window that is clean enough, the new baby is quiet and very bonny, his sister is at the crèche, which we can afford, just about, and no one has to *be* anything, just for now, just for a while.

Apparently, pregnant women aren't as stupid as they think they are. A team of psychologists from the University of Sunderland found that, although many subscribed to the popular view that pregnancy affects your memory and concentration, a series of mental tests showed they actually performed no worse than women who were not carrying a child. Dr Ros Crawley, who headed up the study, said, 'Even though the performance of the two groups did not differ on the cognitive tests, the pregnant women strongly felt that their memory and attention was worse than before they became pregnant.'

So pregnant women are stupid for thinking that they are stupid when they are, in fact, not stupid at all.

Another test says that pregnant women lose ten points off their IQ. I was actually pregnant when I read about this – I forget where, but I was so concerned I went and did an IQ test. I can't remember what the results were. I think they were all right. Maybe I lost the page. Or maybe I just didn't finish the damn thing. I can't remember what happened after that. Oh, I know – I had a baby.

I read somewhere that you lose 3 per cent of your brain *volume* while pregnant. When I asked my obstetrician about this, she laughed and said, 'You never get it back.' Ho, ho, ho.

I know women who do amazing things while pregnant. I was not one of them.

Here is something you do need to know. There is such a thing as antenatal depression, which is to say depression before rather than after the birth. This depression hits in the first trimester of pregnancy when progesterone levels are high, and it predisposes the mother to the ravages of postnatal depression. Women who suffer from PMT, who have a depressive reaction to the pill, or who evidenced a mood disorder at the onset of puberty are particularly vulnerable. And: 'to to 15 per cent of all pregnant women experience what is called antenatal depression, oftentimes severe, sometimes psychotic.'

What I want to know is, how can they tell?

Because the symptoms of pregnancy are, many of them, the same as the symptoms of depression, especially in the first trimester when all you want to do is lie on the sofa. The second time I conceived I went straight to the sofa shop; I said, I am going to spend this pregnancy on a *nice* sofa. Then whoosh, it hit before I could get the credit card out. What is the difference between linen and cotton, between brown and blue? What is the difference between my life now and any other life I might have led? What about leather? Oh, dear, I think I'd better go home and have a little lie-down.

Never mind. Oxytocin, they say – the love hormone, the one that pushes you into labour, the hormone you get while breast-feeding and when you fall in love and also, as a little bonus, during orgasm – this, the world's favourite hormone, also makes you more intelligent. Don't ask me where I read that.

But I do know where I read about the rats – it was on the BBC news website. Female rats that have given birth do significantly better in memory tests than other female rats. Even foster-mother rats performed better than other rodents. That's what we want to hear. 'The mental stimulation of caring for newly born offspring effectively rewires nerve cells and boosts brain power . . . The researchers believe "rich sensory events" generated by caring for young are likely to affect brain structure as well as hormones. The stimulation that comes from suckling in particular probably reorganises connections in a part of the brain called the hypothalamus.'

So it is partly a question of multitasking (changing a nappy while talking on the phone to the Minister of Foreign Affairs), which women were always supposed to be good at, anyway, just as men were supposed to be good at reading maps, and partly something else. Suckling, apparently.

My hypothalamus must be as big as an egg by now. As big as a ping-pong ball. What does your hypothalamus do? I wish they knew.

My mother reared mean multitaskers, both female and male. I was quite good at it, myself, until I had babies. For those first months I am only so so. The most I can manage is a little typing while I breast-feed, and even that is a dreamy, misspelt affair. Otherwise, when I walk down the street I think about the street, when I look at the baby I think about the baby. It is a wordless sort of thinking, mostly, a kind of sea, on which nouns like 'nappy', or 'wind', occasionally drift and bob. 'Whose eyebrows are they anyway?' I say to myself. And, 'Hello!' I say to the baby, 'Hello,' as though we had not met for days.

I wonder, quite often, why they won't all leave us alone. Also why they won't leave the poor rats alone. I wish they would stop feeding rats things in order to give their baby rats two tails or manic depression or poor impulse control. The womb police, I call them. Who are they talking to anyway? They should be petitioning the government over pesticide controls, because there are children born among the wheat fields who have no eyes. They should stand in the hospital out-patients and shout, 'STOP-BEING-POOR!' because poverty is what damages the developing foetus more than anything else. But no, they keep on preaching to the converted, and now that we are all eating our lamb's lettuce and getting our folic acid, they have honed in on those most prevalent of middle-class vices, a cup of coffee and the occasional glass of Chardonnay.

A team in Queens University Belfast discovered that, on one drink per day, foetal response to an external noise at twenty-two weeks was delayed by another week, or more. At the University of Mexico they fed pregnant rats with a 2 per cent, 3 per cent or 5 per cent alcohol liquid diet throughout gesta-tion and found that 'even low to moderate levels of drinking during pregnancy cause long-lasting alterations in synaptic plas-ticity and spatial learning'. I don't call being 2 per cent pissed all day, every day, a low level of drinking, but what do I know? I also think that one drink a day, every day, is very hard going when you are pregnant, even if you are from Northern Ireland, but I suppose they got the women to hold their noses and down it in one. Still, it's not as hard going as the eight cups of coffee per day that a Danish study showed increases the chances of stillbirth by 220 per cent. Eight cups? Who lives like that? Well, lots of people, probably. The world is full of small addictions and necessities. One per cent of women take painkillers every single day, thereby doubling the risk of 'wheeze' in their chil-dren. And if you eat too much peanut butter, you will give them an allergy so severe they go into anaphylactic shock.

Rats who are fed a diet rich in lard are more likely to produce offspring that develop cardiovascular problems, so even those women you meet who put on 70 pounds for the good of the child, retiring to bed every night with a pint of Häagen-Dazs, these, the best-intentioned of all possible women, are harming their children more than they know. It makes you wonder – *should women be allowed to have children at all?* Surely there is a better way.

Or perhaps it is not the scientists – perhaps it is women's fault that we think it is all our fault. When it comes to food guilt, we are quite gleefully neurotic. What we love most is that pause between fork and lip: Should I? Shouldn't I? Oh no, oh dear, unnngggh . . . Gobble gobble munch slurp burp.

When my second baby seemed 'colicky', the advice from other women on the Internet was that, while I was feeding him, I should give up milk, wheat, eggs, citrus fruits, caffeine, chocolate, peanuts, tree nuts, and a very long list of vegetables. As far as I could work out, I could eat brown rice and maybe a little turkey. There was no scientific basis for any of this advice that I could find – except perhaps, in the most distant sense, for cow's milk. Meanwhile, at seven weeks the baby was squawking four hours a night, every night, by the clock. I gave up cow's milk (also, therefore, bread, chocolate, coffee, tea). I lived on brown rice and chanced a bit of fish. The baby stopped crying.

Em. Maybe he had 'peaked'.

These days, what the middle classes worry about most, after autism, is impulse control. Fatty acids, E-numbers; it's not about rickets any more, as much as how to stop them scribbling on the good wallpaper. The middle-class pregnant live on filtered water and grilled wild salmon and too much chocolate ice-cream. And still, there is an overwhelming sense that no matter how properly we reproduce, we are all DOING SOMETHING WRONG! and no one knows what it is. All babies are perfect. They are given to us so that we can wreck them in some tiny but catastrophic way.

Why isn't there a study done about the harm housework does to your unborn child? But scientists rarely research against the interests of industry. They believe in products. Taking vitamins while pregnant, for example, is said to cut the risk of your child contracting neuroblastoma, a particularly horrible and rare kind of tumour, by one-third. Which means that you can take your vitamins, and the child still gets it (bummer). The study does not say what else the mothers were eating. It does not say what toilet cleaner they were using, and how often. It does not say how close they lived to an electricity pylon, or how many of them believed in God, or who had the flu at six months gone. It does not say how many of the children were recovering from their parents' divorce when they developed the cancer, though no doubt these studies will follow, because if there is one thing science loves more than industry, it is a green vegetable, and even more than that, the nuclear family. So we, poor bastards with our weakness for prawn-flavoured Skips and our messy, messy lives, buy the multi-vitamins, and to this act of consumption we cling; or should I say, 'act of purchase', because nobody actually consumes these things, they just leave them in the cupboard until they are past the sell-by date, then go out and buy some more.

Meanwhile, one in every hundred babies born in the US has been involved in a car crash before they see the light of day. One in six pregnant women surveyed in East London had experienced domestic violence during their pregnancy; this study found that 'domestic violence often starts or intensifies during pregnancy', and is 'associated with increases in miscarriage, low birth weight, premature birth, foetal injury and foetal death'. So keep taking the vitamins, girls. Keep taking the vitamins, most especially if you are yourself a child when you have your first child, because 31 births per thousand in Britain are to a mother aged between fifteen and nineteen. And in America 52 per thousand. And in Ireland 53 per thousand.

Sometimes I think scientists and sociologists are just Big Babies. They want mothers to be on hand all day every day and to the child alone. They talk like eight-month-olds with separation anxiety. They talk like toddlers suffering from the unspecified and universal hurt that 'Mother' provokes – because she has left them to go to the shops, for example; or she has betrayed them by having another child; or there is a dog that she pets from time to time; or a book she wants to read; or a television programme that interests her; or any of the things that our babies do not like us to do.

I don't underestimate this anxiety – the idea that a mother can be elsewhere, that she can look at other things, other people, that there *are* other people in the world, leads to only one conclusion: that everyone must die, including the mother, but most especially the Great-I-Am. Children live on the edge, this is why it is important to be as nice to them as you possibly can. But in the same way that toddler insatiability cannot be allowed to run a family, so the unassuageable hunger for the mother cannot be allowed to run society, even if the people who suffer from it are over thirty years old.

Dr Jay Belsky pops up from time to time to give all the working mothers of the world a fright. He is big on the damage that *may* (his italics) be done to children if they are placed in 'non-maternal care' during their first year – which is to say, if their mother goes back to work full-, or even part-, time.

We are all agreed, it seems, that it is both pleasant and important for the mother to be around in a baby's first year – and as many subsequent years, indeed, as we can manage. No one wants us gone. Some countries, like Sweden, even make it possible for mothers to stay at home to look after a new child. What we are not agreed on, what we cannot agree on, is whether, and to what extent, a child is damaged when the mother doesn't spend all her time with it in those first twelve months. We can't agree on it because we can't, many of us, stay at home. We don't have the money. We don't have the patience. But also because we sense that the debate is overblown, that sociology, psychology, or the media's representation of them – *society* perhaps – is just a child pulling at our skirts. The child's need is real, but it is not in some way 'true'. It is not well-founded. Yes, I am leaving – but I will be back in five minutes, or in five hours, and you will be all right. There must be limits to being a mother: not in the spiritual sense, not even in the emotional sense, but between 4.30 and 5.00 on a Tuesday, say, there must be limits to being a mother.

The debate over child care is a debate about a mother's right to work. If there is a risk to the child's development (and this is by no means clear), then it is a risk that many will take, balancing it with the knowledge that so much of our children's happiness depends on our own. Also, that children need good genes, a good father and a deal of money if they are to thrive. Or excel. Or be happy. (Who, by the way, is ever *happy*?) It is not all down to us. In short, it would be lovely if everything was lovely. In the meantime, fuck off.

Dr Belsky says that long-term effects on children who spend more than twenty hours per week in non-maternal care '. . . *may* be associated with diminished compliance and cooperation with adults, increased aggressiveness, and possibly even greater social maladjustment in the preschool and early school years'.

The study used the Strange Situation test. The infant is placed in a room with its mother for three minutes, then a stranger comes in and stays for three minutes, then the mother leaves. Three minutes later she comes back, comforts the child, and leaves it with the stranger again. Then, finally, she comes back for good. Dr Belsky watched for signs of an 'insecure bond' between mother and child – how quickly does the baby stop crying when she picks it up? Also, does the baby push the mother away?

According to this test, 36 per cent of children in child care showed an 'insecure bond' with their mother. Stop press, we have a headline: WORKING MOTHERS DAMAGE THEIR CHILDREN. In the light of which, it is worth saying that 64 per cent of children in child care did not show an insecure bond. Also, that 27 per cent of children who were cared for full-time by their mothers also showed an insecure bond – so I want to know, *What is wrong with the 27 per cent of mothers who stay at home and still don't get it right?*

Actually, what I want to know is what did the Stranger look like? Was it a man? Did he have a beard? (Beards used to make my baby daughter howl.) Was it, even, Dr Belsky himself? But science, of course, never tells you the most important thing.

I misunderstand the whole scientific project, of course. The 27 per cent are not statistically significant, the 36 per cent are statistically significant, and so, by shaving the numbers, we get a curl of 'Truth', that can be verified time after time. So it is some comfort to know that even Belsky could not reproduce his result by using a different attachment test set in a familiar environment, and that there are at least seven other American studies that find no appreciable behavioural difference between children based on their early child care. One Swedish study reports that, at the age of eight, children who had entered child care before the age of one were rated by their teachers as *less* anxious and *more* independent than children who entered child care later or who were cared for full-time by their mothers. But who reported that?

There are women on the Internet who carry their babies around all the time; who never *ever* put them down. It is a fashion. They carry them for every waking moment and then they sleep beside them at night. I do not know how long they do this for – certainly the first twelve months, but maybe more. I do not know how they go to the toilet, or have a shower. But I know that no one is going to make them feel guilty. No one is going accuse them of inadequate mothering. No way.

Meanwhile, may Dr Belsky grow breasts. May he send his children off to college after eighteen years of making their dinners, and cry, and cry.

Babies: A Breeder's Guide

God

It was always a mystery to me why the churches of Ireland were filled with women, and empty of men. I looked up at the crucifix and thought it was a bizarre thing for women to worship a man in a church run by men. As far as I was concerned being a Catholic was silly, and being a Jew meant so much more washing-up. What all religions do, however, is what most political systems fail to do – they prize and praise the figure of the mother.

She is the machine, the hidden power. She is the ideal, the revered one, the truly loved. Which makes up, in a way, for being skipped in shop queues and looking like a heap.

And more. On the third night of my child's life I looked into her eyes and realised that nothing I believed could explain this. It was an embarrassing moment. I think I saw her soul. I suffered from the conviction that a part of her was ancient; and that part chose to be there with me at the beginning of something new. I had a wise child.

Carrying her out of the hospital and into the noise of the traffic; driving her home in second gear; feeding her in the middle of the night, and at the beginning of the night, and at dawn – so precious – I found myself shrinking in the face of her vast and unknowable future. How would she turn out? What would she do? When would she die? Not for many, many years, I hoped; not for the longest time. The mechanisms of fate, the grinding of her days that would lead to one end or another, became urgently opaque to me. There were a thousand things that could hurt this child, or even estrange her from me. What could I do? Nothing. My best.

These are all feelings that religion understands.

I had, I thought, become human in a different and perhaps more radical way. I had let something slip into the stream of time. What else can you do, but trust the river – put it all into the hands of a higher power?

Oh, all right.

And who else, but the suffering Christ, could know the suffering that motherhood brings?

Actually, I will resist the tug of it, if you don't mind. Still, I will resist.

Buggies

All women with buggies look as though they are on welfare. Pushing a buggy makes you look as though you're on the way to the methadone clinic. You look as though you had this baby in a working-class, selfish sort of way – you had this baby even though you couldn't afford a car. A man pushing a buggy looks as though he is someone the global economy left behind. This is why the middle classes have taken to the three-wheeler. People with three-wheelers look as though they go jogging up mountain tracks, whereas in fact, all they do is plonk their fat, post-partum arses behind the steering-wheel of their cars.

Because, even though it folds up, a three-wheeler is too heavy and unwieldy to get on to a bus. You can only get a three-wheeler into the back of a Volvo estate.

In classless America, you can buy buggies in the supermarket for a fraction of the price. They hang them up in rows; ordinary things of plastic and chrome, and dirt cheap. This is because, in America, no one walks, everyone drives.

In Dublin's inner city, on the other hand, you might get a buggy *instead* of a car, they are so fitted and upholstered and sprung; with a milometer and a watch on the broad handle where you park your drink. They have one bit that locks into another bit for all sizes and circumstances, each guaranteed to provoke a nervous breakdown in hissing men and muttering women as they wrestle with straps and clicky bits, and search for the one thing you need to press that no one can find (and meanwhile, who holds the baby?).

In the baby-care shop I am affected by shopping dyslexia. I cannot read these machines. I would put the baby in backwards. I do not know *how* to want a buggy. So we get something simple, in black.

How to buy your first buggy: You have seventeen minutes. You are in tears. You can't go out any more because the baby weighs a ton and your spine is pulled into a question mark by the baby sling you thought would be more appropriate for those early months. But the baby sling makes you feel as though you are monstrously pregnant – only on the outside – and the baby has grown past your chin, so you go to the posh buggy shop and realise just how much poor people spend on their buggies. Then you go to the ordinary buggy shop and get something to match your coat. You put the baby into it. The shop assistant says that they shouldn't be sitting up at that age; she shows you one that allows the baby to lie down, but it is the size and cost of a small house. Besides, it doesn't match your coat. The baby lolls in a roughly seated position in the probably wrong buggy. You pay at the till and say, Can I walk it out? You push the buggy. You experience bliss.

How to get your second buggy: Go to the sales. Get the three-wheeler. Conceive.

Walking along the sea front, my mother takes a turn with the new machine with its glorious suspension and she says, 'Ah, that's more like the way they used to be.' Oh, the satisfaction, and all the pride, of a good pram.

Remember, when you are buying a buggy, that you will pack and unpack this thing four times a day with a possibly scream-ing, and always resentful, baby tucked under one arm. You must be able to fold or unfold whatever you buy with one foot (this is not a joke). There is also the weather and the traffic to contend with, as well as outraged shoppers who think that junkie mothers should be locked up, and some young feller who pushes past you, nearly making you drop the baby, because he is in a hurry and you are taking up too much space, and stopping is not what the street is for.

How to buy your third buggy: Throw out everything; give it away; send it hurtling down a slope into the waters of your local canal; then go and get the lightest, smallest, cheapest thing you can find.

On all three buggies, remember that you must be able to hang your shopping off the back. Sponge handles are always nice, as is the lie-down seat; though a child will doze off in any position, so long as you keep it moving. It is the bumping that does it, or the unscrolling world that confuses them to sleep. Their brain shuts down as they dream of becoming a racing driver, or something else very fast and inexplicable. Buggies are the reason older children take drugs and become joyriders, but who cares? A child could actually live in a buggy most of the time. They love them as a knight might love his horse. A child can also push its own buggy for endless amusement, thus reducing the need for toys.

Walking the streets at 10 a.m., I meet an acquaintance who says, 'Are you still lugging that baby around town?' Perhaps he said, 'toting': 'Are you still toting that child around town?' He might have said, 'dragging'. I look at the baby, her face tight with happiness. She loves being out. She is mad about her buggy. I push on and spend the rest of the day thinking bad thoughts about his sperm count. Build me a house, please, with a split-level living-room and a sprinkler on the lawn. I will live in it with my baby and I will never tote her anywhere again. (Also, fuck you, I will tote her wherever we please.)

Some people don't like children. Some people like children well enough, they just find their mothers annoying, or actually enraging. Especially if they push a buggy. 'Young wans,' one man calls them, complaining about how dangerous we are to cars.

'That's right,' I yelled once at a woman, as she pushed off the kerb and into the path of my bike, 'kill the child, why don't you?' Because women with buggies, as we know, became recklessly pregnant at an early age, so that they can drag their trashy kids around town, while using them to bark the shins of respectable shoppers. Women with buggies do not love their children, they are too busy slapping them at bus-stops, after getting them overexcited with E-numbered sweets. If you want to shop, then you should leave the child with the hired help.

In the bank, a young, eager type of young man slips into the queue ahead of me. It is a neat move: a small weave, and little duck. He is very pleased with himself. He gives me a little smile as though I should be pleased for him, too – all's fair in love and bank queues. I, who have spent two and a half hours trying to get the baby out the door and into town and into the bank before the mortgage is foreclosed, after my fortieth consecutive night of three-hourly feeds, am not pleased for him. I think he should have let me go first. I think the baby may explode before we get to the top of the queue. To stop the baby exploding I push the buggy back and forwards, a little. Push-pull. Push-pull. It is difficult to do this in the confines of the queue, so I step back a little from the smart-arse in front. Push-pull, push-pull, push-pull. At first I don't actually hit him with the buggy, I nearly do. I push the buggy just to the back of his ankles, and think about it. *I hope you have triplets.* Then I tip him a little – just the cloth of his trousers – with the rubber step that slings across the front. Then, I have a bit of a surge, and I do actually hit the back of his leg. Push-pull, push-pull, push-pull. By now he looks quite uncomfortable. Of course, I am just quieting my baby. I am a mother, I don't attack strangers with a buggy containing my cute-looking baby. It must be some sort of absent-mindedness on my part. But when the queue moves forward I move forward too, and I do it some more. Push-pull, push-pull, push-pull. The eager young man looks dead ahead. He doesn't say anything. He is quite right.

Don't mess with me. I am well hard. I have a buggy.

Staring

In the maternity hospital, there are two new parents who look as though they have just survived a war. Grey, shattered; they somehow ignore the smouldering ruins to talk in a very middle-class way into their mobile phones (one each). They look at each other over the receivers, and mouth silently. Then they sign off and say, 'Oh, Gawd, so-and-so is coming in. Well, I couldn't put them off, could I?' They manage to turn it all – the blood, the glory, the raw shock of it – into suburban ennui.

After lunch, the new father leans over the perspex hospital cot to look at his baby. He leans his arms on the end of the trolley and, after a while, slowly hunkers down. As he does so, his trousers ease away from his shirt to show a builder's cleavage of fantastic dimensions. It beams, speakingly, out at the ward, this bosom, as he stares at his baby; not for one hour, not for two, but all the way to tea. The curtain goes over and the curtain swishes back, and he is still there, and his bum is still there: while the mother sleeps, and the baby sleeps. He stares and stares, and continues staring, and even his back-side smiles.

Home Birth

Having a baby is like being run over by a small car – from the inside. Now, if you were facing a small car from the outside, you would certainly make some decisions. Yes, it would help if you lay down. The *position* you adopt is always important. If lying down makes you feel too panicked or helpless, then you might adopt a sitting position, until the very last minute. Some people even recommend moving around until the car is nearly upon you, they say it will help your body take the weight – these are the kind of people who find the experience of being run down by a small car empowering, who recommend yoga to help you relax. If you practise hard, they say, you may feel no significant pain at all.

Sitting, standing or in the lotus position, whatever way you approach it, there is absolutely no need for the old practice of tying you to the road. You are in charge of this. You must, however, breathe out rapidly while a wheel is on your chest or stomach – this is vital. It really does help.

There are those who would prefer to be run over by a small car while under a general anaesthetic – they don't want to see the car, they say, they don't even want to know the colour. But really, it is not a good idea to go all floppy; a certain amount of resistance makes it easier for the motor to get over the hump. It is best to go for something in between – nearly numb, but still able to brace yourself. This is why God invented the epidural – though if the car is coming towards you at speed, it may be too late to ask for one. In any case, some people prefer to be run over quite fast, by a small car. They like to get it over and done with.

Remember that the experience of being run over by a small car is a rare one, and you may want to feel and remember every minute of it for the rest of your life. Some people opt to be run down by a small car in their own home; they find it a more relaxing environment than a cold hospital car park. And really, if you do it properly and don't panic, then there is no cause for concern. Everyone is afraid the car might get stuck, that you might be pinned under the weight of the car for an unspecified length of time. But this is quite silly. Your stomach is designed to take the weight. Your friends and extended family will be there to cheer you on. It will be like a party, the best party you have ever held.

Of course, there is also, and always, the health of the car to consider – this, for me, is the bottom line. It is the main reason that I would never choose to be run over at home.

(Well, that's my story and I am sticking to it. Secretly, and for entirely selfish reasons, if I were to be run over by a small car, then I would like to be near an emergency room, and a fire brigade with some cutting equipment, and also a crane. I would also like a pastel-yellow Mini Metro, please. I'm an old-fashioned sort of girl.)

Wriggles

Babies wriggle. Of all the signals – eyes, smell, the tiny stretch at the height of a yawn, the size of their fingers, and the translucent curve of their ears – a baby's wriggle strikes the keenest note in my mother's heart.

It is so constant, random, and light. Feet and fists rolling in a gentle spasm; it is not yet a squirm. Babies wriggle like puppets, with an incompetent at the strings. There is an occasional panicked jerk of the arms, then the return, in tics and increments, to swaying equilibrium. There is no rest. Babies wriggle exactly as the mechanical babies made for television do, which is why those mechanical babies are so disgusting. In fact, all wriggling things disgust us, make us shriek and fling them away – if they are not babies.

Naming

How do you name a child? I couldn't even name my dolls. Not that I was a dolly sort of girl, but I did get a big plastic job for my fourth birthday that said, 'Mama!' when you turned her upside down. 'What are you going to call her?' said my auntie, and I remember the blankness, the slight panic. What do you call the sky, except 'sky', what do you call a doll, except 'doll' or, at a push, 'Dolly'? The capital letter makes all the difference, and I think I sort of knew this. 'What are you going to call her?' means, 'How will you call her into being?' As if there was a word out there, one simple, magic word, that would bring the plastic alive – if only you knew what it was.

At four years old, I didn't even know where to look. I don't know if children do. It is, I suspect, the adults who decide to call the puppy 'Bobbyfourpence', the children are more than happy with 'Spot'. In the event, my auntie decided on 'Bella'. Why? Because it is the Italian for beautiful, she said. Which made no sense to me at all – I was Irish and the doll was made in Taiwan.

The Chinese for beautiful is, I think, 'Yan', but it is too late to rechristen her now, sitting up in my parents' attic in a pair of gingham knickers, with her voice of plastic perforations fallen out of her back. 'Mama! Mama!' Whose name was she calling? Mine?

A name is not only an incantation, it is also a mark. We mark our children as cute or normal (Trixie, Clare), we mark them as Irish (Síofra), or as middle class (Emma-Louise). It's probably better to go for the social as opposed to the personality choice in all this. The child may not stay cute but it will probably stay Irish (but not *too* Irish, which rules out Gobnait).

And so, we plan. We pat our tummies and try 'Bobby' for size. We cross out all the names of the people we didn't like at school, also former boyfriends, girlfriends, unpleasant colleagues and, in my case, characters from books that I have written, particularly those who were odd or unhappy which, let's face it, most of them were. Strange names are out of the question – it seems that I just want a normal, happy child with a normal, happy name; for which mediocrity of ambition she will, no doubt, come to hate me in time.

And just when I have it figured out, the baby arrives. She doesn't look normal, or even new. She looks extraordinary and ancient and wise. And now I cannot name her, cannot even *know* her, let alone mark her with something so banal as a name. She has an old soul. I look at its benign face, the slow lids batting over the murk of her eyes, and, 'Yoda'! – she is the wrinkled puppet from *Star Wars* who talks backwards. She is the only one. She is 'The Squinch', 'The Baba', 'The Child'. 'Gorgeous!' She begins to smile. You cannot call a child 'Gorgeous', but in the circumstances 'Sarah', for example, is out of the question. Who could call this child 'Sarah', when she might be anyone at all?

And so it begins. 'Thumper', 'Squiggledypop', 'Sweetie-bump', 'Lumdumtious', 'Lamb', 'Baba', 'Babalabaloo'. The gooey litany that keeps our children open for a while, gender-less, unlabelled and free.

I was called 'Funny Foots' because my father used to tweak my toe, apparently, when he came in from work: 'Hello, Funnyfoots.' (I am still quite fond of my feet.) I was also 'Sausage', or even the slightly mouldier 'Fluffy Sausage', also 'Bubbles' and sometimes 'Panzer'. I once asked my father why he called me 'Panzer' – Was it something to do with pansies?

to which, being polite, he said, Yes, neglecting to mention that it was also the name of a fairly large German tank. I was a big girl. Funny how you always remember the jokes that you don't understand – some small smile in the air around your parents, if not exactly on their faces.

My own child now is a 'Little Belter' and I might call her 'Panzer', but that is my own, special tag, and cannot easily be shared. Soon all her names will have settled down to three or four, and I am curious to see what these might be. Because somewhere in me is the ordinary person my parents called 'Anne', but also, and still, the bubbles and the tank. Somewhere in her, perhaps, there will always be the wise child Yoda, as well as the Thumper, as well as the grave and lovely 'Rachel' we finally named her, hopefully, to be.

Burps

At first you think the problem is somehow existential, the baby is lonely, the baby is frightened, the baby is in the dark.

'That baby has wind,' says my mother.

I tell her not to be silly, the baby is too young to have wind. This is a breast-fed baby, how could it be windy? Why should it be so badly designed?

'Oh, I don't know,' says my mother in a voice creaking with resignation. 'That last bit of wind can be very hard to get.' She does not take the baby from me, but later – casually, you might say – she puts it to her shoulder and provokes a seismic belch. The baby screams even louder. I wish she wouldn't do that. I am with the baby on this: I think the wind is my mother's fault.

Two and a half years later, it is four in the morning and the new baby's stomach is hard as a board. I sit him on my knee and hinge his torso forward and back. You might call it rocking, or comforting, but I am actually trying to lever the wind out of him, as simply as if I had a spanner and a wrench. I had forgotten all about this, I was kissing and hugging him and changing nappies like a fool until night three, some hours before dawn, when it all came back in a rush. 'That last bit of wind can be very hard to get.' After which I couldn't get the damn sentence out of my head. Thanks, Ma.

At two weeks I can find the bubble of air with the tips of my fingers and squeeze it out, against the palm of my hand. At a month, I jiggle him on my knee, like getting the fizz out of a bottle of pop. And all the time, there is the hingeing from the hip; the tilt, the rock, the belching jive. From day three, both my babies understood the gravity of all this, and leant into my hand in a solemn, hopeful way.

Burp!

In the queue for his six-week check-up, the baby belches into a room full of new parents, to helpless cries of acclaim and relief.

'Oh, well done!'

'Oh, that's what we like to hear.'

'Uhhh,' says one woman, groaning as though she has been thumped in the stomach, the sound is so good to her ears. We laugh, and night gathers around each of us; the lonely hours we have spent in the various rooms of our various houses, waiting for just that sound.

In my experience, tiny babies cry more often from wind than from hunger – which is to say that they cry more often after food than before it. There are rich metaphysics here, but Freud, for all his talk of the post-orgasmic look on the sated infant's face, has very little to say about wind. Being a genius he could discourse on all our holes – oral, anal, genital – but the burp was just, for him, a remnant: a sign of satisfaction, as you might find in any Bavarian *Biergarten*. He never saw that four-in-the-morning look of utter profundity, as a baby waits on its stomach; thinking about its insides, the volatility of them, how lovely they are and how unfair. You feed a baby and it looks happy, then wary, then aggrieved. After which, the panic rises.

Burp!

Oh, well done!

They always cry louder for a few seconds – it must hurt them, quite a lot – and then they cheer up. After which, a few little possets. After which the hiccups (oh, welcome sound). Then sleep.

You could write a book to this rhythm. You could discuss it all day. How could he miss it? At a guess, Sigmund was not a four-in-the-morning man. At a guess, he was not a man much puked upon.

Hands

There is nothing better, when you can't get up, than lying in bed with a baby. If the baby gets bored, you can flutter your hand, high above its face, then swoop down to beep-beep its nose. If you are very tired, support the waving arm with your other arm, and close your eyes.

Babies love hands. Anyone's hands. Hands make them laugh. They could stare at them and smile at them and play with them all day long. A baby also knows, quite quickly, that it too possesses hands, and that they are the same kind of wonderful object as the mother's. They look from their own fingers to your fingers and back again. Hands!

I find this really exciting. No one else seems to, as far as I know.

Girl / Boy

In the maternity hospital with our baby girl, we are given our first lesson in how to change a nappy. I ask what seems to be a key question; I say, 'What do you do about the crease?' This is, after all, an educational event. The nurse is so embarrassed that she pretends not to hear me; she doesn't even clear her throat. She Moves Swiftly On.

Later, I hear a shriek and settle of women from around one of the nappy tables, like a flock of delighted birds. Another nurse says, 'Well, you can tell he is a real man, anyway' (this is absolutely true). A boy baby has just peed into the Dublin air, in the first year of the twenty-first century, Anno Domini.

Crying

Babies sometimes cry while they are still asleep. This gives them an unfair advantage over their parents, who cannot comfort them without waking up. Though sometimes, it is true, you can feed them and keep dreaming at the same time.

Babies cry for all kinds of reasons. About 5 per cent of the time, babies cry because they have just hit themselves in the face. Later, they cry because they are trying to hit themselves in the face and keep missing. Mostly though, it is wind. And after that, hunger. You would be surprised how often a baby gets hungry. You would be astonished by it. If they are twice as big as last week, it goes without saying that they must be twice as hungry, but sometimes these things sneak up on you. If they are fed and burped, and burped again, then it must be teeth. Or ears. Or colic. Or panic. Or just being tired. Or being too cold. Or being too hot. Or being itchy. Or some neurological thing we don't know about yet.

You can always try holding them upside down. They quite like that, when they are new.

Babies do not go *wa-ah*. In the first days there is an L in the middle of their cry, a helplessness of the tongue as it slaps up to the roof of their mouth. *Ella, ella* – very like the French *hélas*.

Alas! alas! they wail – the tiny ones, just born. *Alas! alas!* from plastic hospital cot to plastic hospital cot. *Alas*.

Or *Hello*. Or *Allah*. *Allah*.

Later the waver goes out of their tongue, and that central L goes nasal; *haNang*. *haNang*. And then, later again, *Aaah-ha*. *Aaah-ha*. *Aaah-ha*. But, in all the years, I have never heard a W in there, except in the broadest sense, when a baby cries through an open grimace, like a Greek tragic mask. The W is more a toddler thing – the wide-mouthed wail, as they struggle to speak through the tears.

'I wa-ah-ah. I waaah. I wan. Hi. Hi. Hi. I waa-ah.'

'What do you want?'

'I wah, I wah, I want a PINK one.'

Babies may say *wa-ah* when they are hysterical, but these days, unless they have colic, you're not really supposed to let them

126

get that far. If they do have colic, you are allowed to set them down. In extreme cases, you are allowed to leave the room, but only in order to take your own medication (you must not medicate the child).

A good trick with crying: hand the baby over to someone who does not love the child. Listen. In their arms, it may not sound so bad. Or it may sound a lot worse, in which case, go for a walk.

When you are on your walk you will hear your baby crying behind every car. You will glance over to the pub, wondering what on earth your baby is doing in there, and why is it crying. You will hallucinate, with utter, almost casual, conviction, the sound of your baby's cry, every three to five minutes.

haNang. haNang. haNang.

A baby's regular cry takes about one second to complete. Inhale-exhale. Inhale-exhale. *haNang. haNang.* Some of it is just idle complaint. 'I smell my dinner, I smell my dinner,' or 'That duck is so yellow, that duck is so yellow,' *haNang. haNang.* Cycling at about a second per cry, it is easy enough to live with – I can take about twenty of them, some people can take even more. But any faster and it becomes unbearable. You have to pick them up. There is always something you can do. Until there is nothing you can do, any more. *haNang. haNang. haNang.*

Time – that's what cures crying. It is also what crying destroys – ten minutes of wails is the longest ten minutes you ever have to undergo. It is six hundred individual complaints, six hundred failures, six hundred rejections, six hundred demonstrations of your helplessness in the face of another's pain.

Let your eyes sink into it. Pause a while.

haNang. haNang. haNang. haNang. haNang. haNang. haNang.

haNang. haNang. haNang. haNang. haNang. haNang. haNang.
haNang. haNang. haNang. haNang. haNang. haNang. haNang.
haNang. haNang. haNang. haNang. haNang. haNang. haNang.
haNang. haNang. haNang. haNang. haNang. haNang. haNang.
haNang. haNang. haNang. haNang. haNang. haNang. haNang.
haNang. haNang. haNang. haNang. haNang. haNang. haNang.
haNang. haNang. haNang. haNang. haNang. haNang. haNang.
haNang. haNang. haNang. haNang. haNang. haNang. haNang.
haNang. haNang. haNang. haNang. haNang. haNang. haNang.
haNang. haNang. haNang. haNang. haNang. haNang. haNang.
haNang. haNang. haNang. haNang. haNang. haNang. haNang.
haNang. haNang. haNang. haNang. haNang. haNang. haNang.
haNang. haNang. haNang. haNang. haNang. haNang. haNang.
haNang. haNang. haNang. haNang. haNang. haNang. haNang.
haNang. haNang. haNang. haNang. haNang. haNang. haNang.
haNang. haNang. haNang. haNang. haNang. haNang. haNang.
haNang. haNang. haNang. haNang. haNang. haNang. haNang.
haNang. haNang. haNang. haNang. haNang. haNang. haNang.
haNang. haNang. haNang. haNang. haNang. haNang. haNang.
haNang. haNang. haNang. haNang. haNang. haNang. haNang.
haNang. haNang. haNang. haNang. haNang. haNang. haNang.
haNang. haNang. haNang. haNang. haNang. haNang. haNang.
haNang. haNang. haNang. haNang. haNang. haNang. haNang.
haNang. haNang. haNang. haNang. haNang. haNang. haNang.
haNang. haNang. haNang. haNang. haNang. haNang. haNang.
haNang. haNang. haNang. haNang. haNang. haNang. haNang.
haNang. haNang. haNang. haNang. haNang. haNang. haNang.
haNang. haNang. haNang. haNang. haNang. haNang. haNang.
haNang. haNang. haNang. haNang. haNang. haNang. haNang.
haNang. haNang. haNang. haNang. haNang. haNang. haNang.

haNang. haNang. haNang. haNang. haNang. haNang. haNang.
haNang. haNang. haNang. haNang. haNang. haNang. haNang.
haNang. haNang. haNang. haNang. haNang. haNang. haNang.
haNang. haNang. haNang. haNang. haNang. haNang. haNang.
haNang. haNang. haNang. haNang. haNang. haNang. haNang.
haNang. haNang. haNang. haNang. haNang. haNang. haNang.
haNang. haNang. haNang. haNang. haNang. haNang. haNang.
haNang. haNang. haNang. haNang. haNang. haNang. haNang.
haNang. haNang. haNang. haNang. haNang. haNang. haNang.
haNang. haNang. haNang. haNang. haNang. haNang. haNang.
haNang. haNang. haNang. haNang. haNang. haNang. haNang.
haNang. haNang. haNang. haNang. haNang. haNang. haNang.
haNang. haNang. haNang. haNang. haNang. haNang. haNang.
haNang. haNang. haNang. haNang. haNang. haNang. haNang.
haNang. haNang. haNang. haNang. haNang. haNang. haNang.
haNang. haNang. haNang. haNang. haNang. haNang. haNang.
haNang. haNang. haNang. haNang. haNang. haNang. haNang.
haNang. haNang. haNang. haNang. haNang. haNang. haNang.
haNang. haNang. haNang. haNang. haNang. haNang. haNang.
haNang. haNang. haNang. haNang. haNang. haNang. haNang.
haNang. haNang. haNang. haNang. haNang. haNang. haNang.
haNang. haNang. haNang. haNang. haNang. haNang. haNang.
haNang. haNang. haNang. haNang. haNang. haNang. haNang.
haNang. haNang. haNang. haNang. haNang. haNang. haNang.
haNang. haNang. haNang. haNang. haNang. haNang. haNang.
haNang. haNang. haNang. haNang. haNang. haNang. haNang.
haNang. haNang. haNang. haNang. haNang. haNang. haNang.
haNang. haNang. haNang. haNang. haNang. haNang. haNang.
haNang. haNang. haNang. haNang. haNang. haNang. haNang.
haNang. haNang. haNang. haNang. haNang. haNang. haNang.

haNang. haNang. haNang. haNang. haNang. haNang. haNang.
haNang. haNang. haNang. haNang. haNang. haNang. haNang.
haNang. haNang. haNang. haNang. haNang. haNang. haNang.
haNang. haNang. haNang. haNang. haNang. haNang. haNang.
haNang. haNang. haNang. haNang. haNang. haNang. haNang.
haNang. haNang. haNang. haNang. haNang. haNang. haNang.
haNang. haNang. haNang. haNang. haNang. haNang. haNang.
haNang. haNang. haNang. haNang. haNang. haNang. haNang.
haNang. haNang. haNang. haNang. haNang. haNang. haNang.
haNang. haNang. haNang. haNang. haNang. haNang. haNang.
haNang. haNang. haNang. haNang. haNang. haNang. haNang.
haNang. haNang. haNang. haNang. haNang. haNang. haNang.
haNang. haNang. haNang. haNang. haNang. haNang. haNang.
haNang. haNang. haNang. haNang. haNang. haNang. haNang.
haNang. haNang. haNang. haNang. haNang. haNang. haNang.
haNang. haNang. haNang. haNang. haNang. haNang. haNang.
haNang. haNang. haNang. haNang. haNang. haNang. haNang.
haNang. haNang. haNang. haNang. haNang. haNang. haNang.
haNang. haNang. haNang. haNang. haNang. haNang. haNang.
haNang. haNang. haNang. haNang. haNang. haNang. haNang.
haNang. haNang. haNang. haNang. haNang.

And you are involved with each *haNang*, you understand. You dip and lift, and do your best six hundred times. At each breath your mind surges with sympathy and a pleading that is barely articulated.

There there. There there. There there. You're all right. You're all right. You're all right. That's it, oh, there, that's it, that's it. That's it, that's it, that's it. Oh, shush now, please stop, yes, stop, do stop, please. You're all right. You're all right. You're all right. There there. There there. There there. That's it. That's it. Please stop, hush, hush, oh, please. There there. There there. You're all right. You're all right. You're all right. That's it, shush, that's it, that's it. Oh, that's it, oh, there, that's it, that's it. Oh, please stop, yes, stop, shush, shhhh. You're all right. You're all right. You're all right. There there. There there. There there. Shush now.

Until you break into speech with a rhythmic groaning as the baby is bounced on your shoulder, adding your own *uhHung. uhHung. uhHung. uhHung* to the monotony of its distress. After which you might rise to the shush itself, that most irritating sound, *Sssss. Sssshhh. Shush. Ssss* or the falling song of *Doh! doh doh do do. Doh! doh doh do do. Doh! doh doh do do.* Or even a real song, gasped at speed, then slowly deepened into its true lyrical–tragical version as in 'Bob . . . the . . . builder . . . Can . . . we . . . fix . . . it?' which becomes quite moving, really, when you repeat it twenty-seven times. All of which will cover the first five minutes, after which there is another five minutes to go.

The worst, in my experience, is the tired-feed-burp cycle. This happens when you try to knock a baby out by feeding it, and end up giving it wind instead. A tired baby knows what it wants and it does not like to be thwarted, but because food is very *like* sleep to the wanting baby, you deliver another liquid cosh, after which you have to burp it again and so on, until it becomes too enraged to fall asleep, and you give it more food, until . . . until . . . until . . . I don't know what happens in the end. They must fall asleep. No one is still awake at the age of twenty. Are they?

I don't know.

It is like when you are in the middle of toilet training and there is misplaced shit, and secret shit, and helpless shit on various surfaces about the home that were not designed to take it, like for example the handle of the phone, and people say, as you hurl the receiver away from you, 'Don't worry, no one ever went to college in nappies.' And what you want to shout back is, *Are you sure?*

Still, time does pass. The wind eases, the world becomes less alarming, the baby learns how to want in a simpler way, as you learn how to supply. And, just when you think you are through the worst of it, the baby starts teething, or it gets an ear in-fection, or it forgets how to go to sleep; or it starts getting lonely, especially at night.

At some stage towards the end of the first year, we all try what is called 'controlled crying'. This involves leaving a baby to cry for more than thirty seconds at a time. Actually, you are supposed to leave the baby for as many minutes as it has months, and then increase it, or decrease it, or something. It mostly means fathers tying mothers to some solid piece of furniture and saying, 'It's fine, the baby is fine.'

The baby is manifestly not fine. In this scenario, as the baby lies there and the crying escalates and turns to rage, and cranks up to raw panic, and then hits a wild note that sounds like guilt to me (what have I done, to be so abandoned?) I have only one question. At this precise moment, who hates who the most? Does the mother hate the father more than the father hates the baby? Does the father hate the mother more than the mother hates the father? Does she hate him more than she hates the baby? Does no one hate the baby? Who does the baby hate? Does no one hate anyone? Why is everyone screaming, now? Answers on a postcard, please.

If it is the mother who leaves the baby to wail, saying for

instance, 'It doesn't make any difference what I do,' then it may be time to bring the mother to the doctor. Or it may just be a passing thing she is going through; a Tuesday thing, that is gone by Wednesday afternoon.

None of this is true for the second baby, by the way. You put a second baby into the cot and the second baby turns on to its side and goes to sleep. Then you go to sleep. It is just as you suspected – it was all your fault in the first place.

Both my babies were very moderate criers. I had this theory about panic. I thought, if you let them panic in their first days, then that will be the way their brains are made. I decided that if you give the first three months to a baby, entirely and without stint, then it will reward you by being easy for the rest of its life.

Of course, people with theories should, at all times, be scorned. And instead of 'months', I should have said 'decades'.

Why do we assume that babies are happy in the womb? They come out looking for your face, so who is to say they are not lonely, all those weeks when there is no face there? And maybe their guts are at them, maybe the bones of their face ache from the early beginnings of teeth; maybe growth itself hurts, in the womb, as it does outside, and all that squawking in the early weeks is not a mourning for paradise lost, but just making up for lost time.

Evolution

I have a few new theories for the evolutionary sociologists, that pack of intellectual baboons.

133

1) Men went out to hunt because if they didn't bring home a
dead antelope their pregnant women would eat them in the
middle of the night. She wakes up. She suffers a nameless
hunger. She sees a nice bit of leg.

2) Why do we give birth in pain? Humans give birth in pain
so that they can't run away afterwards.

Authority

At the baby's six-week check-up, the paediatrician lies her
down on the couch and drifts away from her. This woman
moves in slow motion. She gives out no signals; she is so
calm and contained that I cannot tell where she is, behind
me in the room. This is what happens when you work with
sick babies all the time. Beside her we are massively over-
wrought. This is our baby, please tell us that she is all right
(of course the baby is all right – just look at her). Please tell
us that we are doing it properly. Please do not take her from
us, even for a minute, even behind a screen. I pick the babygro off one sleeve at a time. The baby does not cry. Is this
good? Perhaps she should cry. In the white towelling there
is an errant pubic hair that must have come from our bed.
It is a deeply shocking pubic hair. The paediatrician bends
over the baby and moves her limbs, then she obliges us to
make her smile. Then she says that we have a happy, healthy
baby. Then we give her forty-five pounds. We would have
given her four thousand five hundred. We would have given
her anything.

Poo

Babies need you to smile at them when they are feeding and also – and more urgently – when it is coming out the other end. This is what the rest of the world has to come to terms with. Often, when a mother is whispering to a baby, she is whispering about shit.

'Oh, go on then,' says one woman, lovingly. 'Have a good poo.'

We keep our voices light, our tone of voice adoring.

'Have you a secret in your nappy?' coos another woman, 'Have you a little present for me?' We nuzzle and agree and admire. We help them along, as though they were doing something delicate and sweet and difficult, like blowing the seeds off a dandelion clock.

'There you go!'

This is probably all necessary to the child's mental health. But still – I don't know. Is this where that dreadful female impulse comes from, to put little crocheted dollies over the toilet rolls?

Smell

In order to wash a tiny baby's hair, you have to wrap them up and turn them upside down, often in the bathroom sink, often with someone else whimpering outside the door, saying, 'Careful.' Really, there is not much point in washing a tiny baby's hair, and so you get the nostalgic smell of scalp that is soap-free. A baby's hair smells keenly of humanity. It makes people groan, small but deep – a kind of creaking in their gut as they inhale and say, 'Hmmm.'

Babies smell of rusks, even if they don't eat them. Tiny babies smell like kissing someone in a field: also of milk, and asparagus, and – it's up to you really – pancakes cooked in the Frytex of your youth; baby lotion, even if they are wearing none; sunshine, even in the middle of winter; and so on. They smell of all lost things, now regained.

Babies' feet smell, bizarrely, of feet. It starts early.

Babies' shit smells a little like ham going off. Also biscuits. Sometimes, if their tummy is upset, there is a whiff of fried egg. One day, much later, you turn from the nappy table and say, 'Christ, that actually smells like shit.'

Babies' earwax smells like earwax, from the word go. It creeps out a week after they are born and makes you wonder if there is not some amniotic remant in there; some crease in the baby in which a part of you is still lodged. But no, it is earwax. The real thing. My goodness, everything works!

Babies finally smell like you and they smell like your partner. This is as it should be. This was the way they are made. But I wonder if they don't just take our imprint on to their skin, which is to say, the imprint of the last person to hold them – the mother's, the father's, the baby-minder's, the woman in the doctor's waiting-room who asks can she 'have a go'. Some parents can smell a stranger off their baby as soon as they pick them up – I am speaking of quite normal parents here – they can smell musty old talc, and women who wear Obsession, and the baby-minder's car with its little bottle of aromatherapy oil, plugged into the place where the cigarette lighter used to go.

Perhaps babies are just olfactory blotting paper. They smell of the person who last minded them. They smell of You.

What do we do with babies? We inhale them, our face hovers over them, we hold them and keep a tiny, delicious distance between their skin and our own. We kiss them thoughtfully on the crown of the head, and we kiss them playfully in the fat, soft cushion under the chin. All day, we sniff them up and down. We do not lick them.

Too Much Information

Yes, it is possible to breast-feed if you have cosmetic implants. In fact, the silicone used by cosmetic surgeons, methyl poly-dimethylsiloxane, has a structure very similar to that used in a popular remedy for colic, simethicone – which binds with the minute bubbles of air in the baby's gut, joining them together to make bigger bubbles, for the easier burp experience.

Bonus.

Baby-talk

What used to be called baby-talk is now called 'parentese'. It used to be frowned on as exceptionally silly and dangerous, but now, if you want your child to grow up to be a genius you *talk iida ickle baba like dis* for the first . . . well, they don't say, actually. How Long? How Long O Lord? are we supposed *iid talk to de a baba ike dis, yes, we ARE! How long do we have to? Yes, how long wong?* Fifteen years maybe? For fifteen years we talk to our children, *Yes, We Do! like this!* We say, *Don't take those nasty druggy-wuggies!* We say, *Don't stay too late at the dancie dancie. At the wave.*

Long ago, in another life, I was a media hack, chasing a story in Dublin town. It was a serious story, a complex story, a story about corruption, graft, injustice. We were driving along, chewing it over, when my fellow hack, my co-hack, you might say, said, *Oh! Look at the big GREEN bus.* What can you do? Nothing. We threw our fag-ends out of the window and stepped on the gas. That night . . . she did a lot of overtime.

She couldn't help it. Children are actually a form of brainwashing. They are a cult, a perfectly legal cult. Think about it. When you join a cult you are undernourished, you are denied sleep, you are forced to do repetitive and pointless tasks at random hours of the day and night, then you stare deep into your despotic leader's eyes, repeating meaningless phrases, or mantras, like *Ooh da gorgeous. Yes, you are!* Cult members, like parents, are overwhelmed by spiritual feelings and often burst into tears. Cult members, like parents, spout nonsense with a happy, blank look in their eyes. They know they're sort of mad, but they can't help it. They call it love.

Or is it just mothers? See that man walking down the street? He's a New Man. He has his child in a sling. Every woman he passes smiles at him. Every woman he passes wants to have him and the baby, now – the complete package, no hassle, no nine months. Does he talk to the child? Does he *gaa* and *goo*? Certainly not. He has an image to maintain. He'll talk into his mobile walking down the street, he'll even talk into a hands-free mobile that makes him look as though he's talking into thin air, but he'll wait until he's in the door, until the door is safely closed, until the door is locked, before he does the *tickle ickle wid de baba, yeah.*

I know a guy who says they can't understand sarcasm until

the age of eight. So he goes, *Oh you are so wonderful!* in a voice that is very close to horrible. But maybe baby-talk is, by its nature, very close to horrible, very close to completely insincere.

They have studied baby-talk and pulled it apart and called it parentese, and apparently it's all about vowel sounds. The three vowels, Ah, Eeh and Oh, are like the prime colours of speech – all other vowel sounds are a mixture of these three basic ones, and these are the ones we elongate when we are talking to our babies. Repetition, which is one of the main components of parentese, makes it more easy-weasy for the baby to hear the vowels, with its sweet ickle eary ears. Consonants, meanwhile, become softer and thicker. We lose the L, and turn Th into D. I'm not sure why that is. I should, I suppose, look up my Chomsky-Womsky, or some other experty-werty, but I am afraid they will tell me that long vowels are all very well, but I am a Bad Mama! for distorting consonants and, even worse, replacing the pronouns with silly-billy nouny-wouns.

But of course some other expert would say that silly-billy nouny-wouns are absolutely essential for your baby's development, and all those old duffers, who hate the sound of baby-talk, are just . . . embarrassed. As some people are. Embarrassed by joy. Excluded. Jealous.

Actually the best thing about baby-talk is the way people use it to talk about the other people in the room. They say, 'Did your Mammy put you down on that dirty old ruggy-wug?' They say, 'Who's that big nasty man with the tight old botty-wot, doesn't like the way we talk. Isn't he a silly-billy? Isn't he a silly old moo?'

The Killing Cup

I am eight and a half months' pregnant, and in a taxi. The driver is a woman. She isn't a great talker but suddenly, in a rush, she tells me about the cup of tea that killed the baby. She just has to warn me. The mother spilt it, apparently.

'It wasn't even that hot.'

My own mother knows of many children killed in freak accidents – some as recently as 1953. Every time she starts with one, I tell her about the granny who pushed the buggy off the kerb while on holiday, not realising that they drove on the other side of the road in France. And besides, it only happened in 1998.

I may mock.

Each of us has our baby tragedy. I like the one about the toddler who walked out of her mother's bed in the middle of the winter in Canada and fell asleep in the snow, wearing nothing but a nappy. She was revived some hours later, or so the news report went, with no appreciable damage to her brain. It was a kind of cryogenics, apparently. It only works if you are small. The mother, who contributed in this significant way to the sum of scientific knowledge, was 'too shocked to comment'.

Martin remembers the man whose wife rang him from the nursery, to ask where the child had been all day. The man leapt from his desk and ran down to the car park, where he found the baby still in the back seat of the car. Unfortunately it had overheated and died. This story was in the newspaper.

There is no worse trap than a car. Children play with the cigarette lighter and burn the whole tin box down. People are always stealing the things without looking around to check if there is a baby in the back. This is because parents leave the keys in the ignition to keep the heating or the air-conditioner going, while they, for example, nip into the shop. In Dublin last week, a drug addict was sent to jail for stealing a car that contained two small children and a baby. He let the children out in a hospital car park and, when a woman came over to see why they were crying, he ordered them all back in. Then he drove away again.

This means that, either you have to take the keys out of the car when you go up to pay in the petrol station, or you have to take one, two, or more children out of the back of the car and into the shop, whether they are asleep or not. Or you can just fling your money down on the forecourt and leave.

Now, people may think it bonkers that a parent cannot leave his or her child in the back of a car in order to go and pay for petrol. What they don't realise is that, no matter how outlandish the accident, it is about to happen to *your* child, now. There is an entire American literary tradition built on just this fact.

I used to think that people are more relaxed in the third world where, apart from starving, they have less on their mind. But this idea was given the lie by a friend who came back from working in a Filipino village, and said that the place was full of fretful hypochondriacs, prone to impatience and panic, just like anywhere else. In fact, he said, being poor makes you more stressed and certainly more fearful for your children, even though they have more children to, as it were, play with.

I find this terrifying. The idea that if you have nine children you end up nine times as worried — it can't be possible. You would explode. Surely you have more children partly in order to allay your anxieties about the first. You should be nine times *less* worried about each individual child. (Ah, but what if you all died in the same train crash?) The sad fact seems to be that there is no maths to it. The family is not a bucket you can fill up to a certain point, and then carry around without slopping the water out. Or something.

Actually, I suspect there is no metaphor to describe the family – what it is, and how it works. The family is the origin of metaphor, not its end point. But whatever way you fail to describe what a family is, there is no doubt that parents are (delightfully) crippled by it. This is why allowances must be made: we are not human beings who can walk around and do as we please, we are human beings with strange, sometimes quite large, extra bits of flesh attached, and each extra bit has desires of its own.

Parents should be treated with every possible consideration. There should be someone at the petrol pump to take their money. There should be a supermarket without sweets. There should be pigs flying around for free, to take us all for a ride on their backs.

Where was I?

Now that I have two children, I am particularly drawn to the story of the toddler who put his new sibling into the tumble-drier, because its nappy was wet. The mother was asleep upstairs at the time. The baby died.

I can taste that sleep. I can fall into it. I can imagine how tired she was, how gorgeous it was to close her eyes – this woman who will never sleep again.

Kissing

I am not kissing my baby, I am checking its temperature.

How to Panic

The baby patters in with an open bottle of children's paracetamol in her hand, stretched out for me to see. It is first thing
in the morning. Her father has changed her nappy and gone
to work and I am still lying there like a stone – so I deserve
this. This is my fault.

'Give the bottle to Mama.'

It looks full enough. There is maybe a quarter gone. Maybe
less. At eighteen months she is still teething and running a
temperature, so she had two, perhaps three, spoonfuls. I look
at the label. I hold the bottle up to the light. There could not
be more than 25 ml gone. Which means she could not have
taken more than 5 ml and that's all right, isn't it?

It is at this moment that my mind shuts down.

My thoughts are, for the most part, banal and perversely
social (what will the neighbours think if her liver fails?) but
they are not sane. I can hear the story in my head: *Someone
must have left the cap off. The bottle was still beside the cot.* So I
tell myself – and it is a very clear form of instruction, this; I
am standing by the window staring at the bottle and address-
ing myself, sternly but kindly, as you might a child – I tell
myself that there is no danger, there is no need to panic. Then
I tell myself that this is exactly the sort of situation in which
you are supposed to panic, *even if* there is no danger you must
also panic, you are A Mother now, these substances are
Dangerous, you must not be afraid to Seek Help, you MUST
PANIC.

I ring my sister, partly because she is a doctor but mostly
because she is the only person in Dublin who will answer
her mobile phone. My sister's mobile phone saves lives.

Unfortunately she is in the middle of saving someone's life when I ring, so she says 25 ml sounds fine, but she doesn't know the dose for weight (or something) for childhood para-cetamol and tells me to ring the poison helpline. She says she doesn't know the number, and then she gives me a number anyway, which I ring. A woman answers and I say, 'My daugh-ter has taken some paracetamol, at least I think she might have taken some paracetamol, it is the children's stuff, Calpol, she's a year and a half, she's 29 pounds, she's taken maximum 20 or 25 ml but I don't really know.' I am being very specific. I am only giving the information that might, medically, be required. I cannot understand why the woman at the other end of the phone has started to laugh. I start to falter and she says, 'I'm only the exchange.' I say, 'Could you put me through to some-one in the poisons unit, then?' and she says, 'No! No, I can't!' She is still laughing. She thinks this is hilarious. I put the phone down.

Through all this the child looks at me with quiet interest. And indeed she does look fine, I am not so much worried about her as about this phantom other – the girl who, by tragic accident, by neglect, by the fact that her mother sleeps late, is already in an advanced state of liver failure (and none of this matters either, you know, the sleeping late – the details and coincidences, the whole story and who is to blame. If the child is harmed, if anything happened to the child, then there could be no cause to explain this too-large result.).

I put the baby into the car, without her breakfast, and we go down to the clinic. The receptionist goes into the doctor's room holding the bottle of paracetamol high, like a urine sample, in front of her. Then she comes out of the doctor's room and gives it back to me. The doctor has said something wry or

144

dismissive. The receptionist is swallowing her amusement anyway and, quite kindly, she tells me to go away now, everything is fine.

The thing is, I knew it was fine all along. My sister rings later and I tell her about the woman who laughed at me on the phone. She says the number she gave me was for Directory Enquiries. She, too, nearly laughs at me, but then she doesn't. We all know what it is like to be that stupid – we all know what it is to shut down, to stop existing for one moment, standing by a window, for example, with a bottle of Calpol in your hand. And then, an hour, or a week later, when someone has shouted long and loud enough that everything is all right, we say, 'Oh,' and walk on.

Romance

The baby falls in love with her father.

Her father is *over there*. Her mother, on the other hand, is simply here. She crawls over me like some well-loved cushion, she meets my gaze and holds it for the longest time: she looks *into* me, but she looks *at* her father. He is a wonderful object, and watching at him makes her radiant with pleasure.

Mind you, he is usually doing something very watchable; he might be throwing a toy into the air, for example, to catch it behind his back.

'Silly Dada,' I say.

The Lip of the Rug

It is often something small – the thing you will never forget. A woman looks down, as she is running from child-minder to child-minder, and sees blisters on her hands from pushing the buggy. Another woman remembers the lip of the rug – nights of pushing the child over and back, over and back, and there is something so keen and total in the tiny thump and lift of the wheels: how did her life, with all its particular importance, shrink to this quarter-inch? To the line between a rug and the parquet. How can your life be reduced to a raw sac of skin on the mound of your thumb? Twenty years later this woman lifts her hand to show me exactly where the calluses formed; like a man shot in a war that no one wants to remember any more.

By the Time You Read This, It Will be True

A Hollywood celebrity has hired a lactation expert to incorporate her breast milk into her diet. 'She spends 570 calories a day producing milk, if she then consumes those calories back again, she has knocked 1,000 calories off her total, right there. Theoretically it is possible to live on negative calories, which is to say, less than nothing – you can starve the system while still consuming 500 calories a day, which is sort of interesting to think about, but we don't really recommend it.' Asked how the breast milk was consumed, the Beverly Hills $1,000-a-day consultant said, 'We do a range of products. A lot of it ends up in the salad dressing. You'd be surprised.'

Staring, Part 2

A friend of mine, who is a mother, says, 'I will never forget the day that he looked right through me.' She indicates where he was sitting, twelve years ago, in his nappy, on the floor. She points it out on the tiles. What did he see, when he looked right through her? She cannot really say. Transparency. A chill wind.

'Who are you?'

Another woman says, 'I wasn't feeding him fast enough and he knocked the spoon out of my hand, and the look he gave me was absolutely evil.' This woman has postnatal depression – but still, what was that look? I want to know. I want to know what message passed between the baby and his depressed mother. Sometimes I think we are only mirrors of each other, that you give birth to a flesh-and-blood mirror, one that can turn to you, or away from you. A mirror that bites. A mirror that grows.

And this is nonsense too, because we read more into babies than they (perhaps) give out. There should be another language for babies. Adult words carry too much baggage, they are too social and burdened with intent. How could a baby be 'evil' or even just 'smug'. And later, how can we say that they 'flirt', or 'manipulate' or even 'know' you? They are not in charge. To a large extent, a baby just 'is'.

So when you look into a baby's eyes, you look into something for which there are no words. This is love. This is what love always feels like. To look into someone's eyes and find words failing.

Still, you need to be in the full of your mental health to suffer a baby's stare.

What's Wrong with Velcro?

You will spend ten minutes every day on socks. Finding socks, matching socks, putting socks on the baby, returning down the supermarket aisle to pick up fallen socks, putting socks back on the baby's foot. Washing socks. Fishing socks out of the drier. Matching socks. All this for something that lasts five minutes on the actual baby's actual foot. Babies' feet are not designed for independent footwear.

So I decided against socks. Ten minutes a day is over an hour a week. That's more than fifty-two hours in the first year. You could spend a full working week on socks. I can't afford a week's extra, unpaid, sock holiday. Never mind the money – *emotionally* I can't afford to spend a week of my life on socks. So I put the baby in babygros, because babygros made sense. After a while, though, as she got bigger and then very big indeed, they made her look like a paradoxically slow developer and I realised that it was time to enter the world. It was time to buy trousers and dungarees that open all down the legs, and tights (have you ever tried to get a wriggling baby into a pair of tights?) and socks. It was time to fiddle with fasteners and curse over funny-shaped buttons, match pink with purple and purple with blue, and still have the child's arse hanging out after half an hour, when all the poppers have popped and the tights drooped, and her dinner is splashed all down her front.

You see that cute baby in a buggy, with a little stretchy hair band and embroidered sandals and an ironed dress that really does not appear to have shit on it, no matter which way you turn it round? That baby represents, in terms of shopping, washing, ironing – I don't know, half a day? No, a whole day's work.

★

My mother attacks the baby with a wet hanky.

'Did you spit on that?' I say and she is quite shocked.

'I'd never spit on a hanky.'

'Oh, how quickly we forget,' I say, and we are arguing the toss while the baby squirms away from the scrubbing finger that I remember so well.

My father watches for a while, and then he says, 'Why do women always have to be *polishing* them?'

Being a man, he would rather a baby go mucky. He would rather walk down the street with a baby whose face is smeared in porridge, Jaffa Cake and snot, than make a baby cry. He has no shame.

Then again, there is nothing so beautiful as a clean child. All that fresh skin. They do scrub up wonderfully well.

'Its very low-grade work,' I say to one woman, who asks after the baby and how I am finding it all. She turns on me, horrified.

'Rearing children is one of the most emotionally and intellectually taxing jobs there is,' she says (or something like). Well no, actually. Or maybe rearing them is, but keeping them clean and cleaning up after them is not, and much of your time is spent doing just that. And yes, I have tried letting the baby hold the dustpan, while I ply the brush. As far as I am concerned, rearing a baby means holding, smiling, feeding, shushing and waving a rattle around. This can be lovely, but it is sometimes quite dull, and the rest is pure drudgery. The only intellectual challenge, in the midst of such ecstatic inanity, is how to keep yourself sane. (Rearing a toddler – now for that you need brains.)

Even so, there are things that are much more intellectually taxing, like *Scrabble*. And there are things that you will never be able to learn. Like patience. I would swap several college degrees for a degree of patience. And much more important than a good brain is a good washing machine. If your washing machine broke down you would never be found again; they would have to send out a search party; they would have to dig out your body from under a drift of dirty clothes.

Tip: On the weekend, one partner can stay by the door of the washing machine while the other dresses and redresses children and adults, as they become spattered and respattered with one or other digestive product. The first partner will then load, unload and reload them into various washers and driers, also into the disinfecting buckets for pee and poo, then unload them finally and fold them. No one will ever put them away. On Sunday, you can swap places.

Clean, dirty, wet, dry, ironed or wrinkled, and always insidiously stained; you will drown in clothes. Between presents, hand-me-downs and impulse buys, a nonsense of clothes. Every colour you would never wear yourself; you have to put on sunglasses just to find the zipper. They will all be the wrong size. Or they will be the right size but the wrong season. For the three hot days of any given summer, you will have seven dresses – two are too small, two are too big, two are too tarty and the lovely one costs too much to actually wear.

Or maybe not. Maybe you will do all this bit much better than me.

Newborn babies' clothes should be as disposable as nappies. Babies grow like pumpkins – they can skip a whole size overnight. Some of their clothes will never get worn twice and many will never be worn at all. The wisest thing is not to bother washing them, just throw them out as you go, without a backward glance. Yes, all the pretty embroidered cotton dresses, and the cutie-pie hats, the dungarees with 'Woof' written on the front – into the bin with them. The ordinary bin. The one that goes to the dump.

Otherwise you will spend the next many years moving them from one cardboard box to another cardboard box. You will build heaps of clothes for local charities, heaps for foreign charities, heaps that are too good for poor people, that you want to save for the children of friends. Then you will move them from one pile to another. Why should poor children not wear designer clothes? Why should Africans not need jumpers – does it not get cold in the mountains of Rwanda?

Then you will pause and rub your face in some tiny dress or trousers, and lay it gently down, realising as you do so that you can never give away this shred and remnant of your happiness, your baby's first weeks, or first year, or decade. You can never give it away because you still don't believe it – any of it – you need proof that they were once so small.

And so it goes. Your children will have, at any given time, three times as many clothes as you do. If you have a daughter, most of these clothes will be pink, even if, like me, you wear black all the time. (When the sun is shining, I might lighten up to brown, but hey, that's the kind of glamour puss I am.) I quite like dark colours on children, but to dress a girl in black would, these days, be considered almost criminal. It must glow. It must dazzle. You must participate in the pink thing, the frilly thing, the floral thing, the pretty-pretty thing or you will endanger their mental health. You must consume. So I say, Go the whole hog and just throw the damn things in the bin, after they've been worn twice. Or do it before you take it out of the wrapping, to save time. Why don't they have bins right there in the shop? Society operates at the level of the three-year-old, because there is no greater consumer than a three-year-old, but I resent the idea that buying endless, useless things for your children is good for them. I resent the way that small girls are complimented on their clothes by everyone, all the time, *unceasingly*, when there are so many other things that people could praise. Despite which, of course, I buy things all the time. Bring on the endless, meaningless, sweatshop, frilly bits, that's what I say; we must have them, the bad-karma runners and the pink wellingtons made in some country that never sees rain. Dress them up and dress them down.

When the baby went down to the crèche after her first birthday, they looked at her bare feet and enquired about socks and shoes.

'Oh, she doesn't wear shoes,' I said. 'She just doesn't like them.' Poor child. When she finally got a pair on her feet she took off like Arkle, over grass and gravel.

Unforgiven

These are the things for which children (eventually) forgive their fathers:

Going out.
Coming home late.
Smelling of drink.
Reading the newspaper.
Watching the television.
Looking at people on the television with a vague sexual
    interest.
Not being bothered, much.

Having other important things to do.

These are the things for which children never, ever, ever forgive their mothers:

Going out.
Coming home late.
Smelling of drink.
Reading the newspaper.
Watching the television.
Looking at people on the television with a vague sexual interest.
Not being bothered, much.
Having other important things to do.

When I was in my teens and twenties, it was fashionable among girls to complain about your mother – despite the fact that these women had given their lives over to rear us. It was never fashionable to complain about your father, unless they were very drunk, all the time. At worst, fathers provoked a shrugging silence – presumably because this was what they gave.

So what about New Men? Will we need a new psychology in twenty years for children, now grown up, whose fathers were there half the time, who changed the nappies and sang the lullabies, half the time, or more? Is it possible that in twenty years or so we will find it is the caring father, and not the caring mother, who is ultimately to blame?

I doubt it.

I have met some of these maligned mothers since and it is great fun having a look at them. Some of them, to my surprise, really do seem wretchedly ungiving. But most of them are quite nice. Or ordinary. Or even dull.

A dull mother? There is no such thing. It is odd that, as a group, mothers are seen as a lardy wodge of nothing much; of worry and love and fret and banality. As individuals we are *everything*. Between these two extremes, where does the person lie?

In my thirties and forties, many of the daughters who gave out about their mothers started going shopping with them, talking about kitchen units, doing all the things that friends might do and more, while the mothers – I don't know what the mothers did, exactly, but they shifted too. They let their children be. The battle was over. As though each side had fought its way into the light of day and looked at each other to find . . .

Now that I have become a mother myself, it is a great comfort to me to see how most of us come to an accommodation between the 'MOTHER!' in our heads and the woman who reared us. The whole process reaches a sort of glorious conclusion if and when the daughter has children herself. 'Now you understand,' says the (grand)mother. 'Now you see.' This is what they yearn for – as much as any adolescent, they need to be understood. They need an end to blame.

I take the baby home, and watch my parents with different eyes. My father likes looking at small children – just that. He hates disturbing them, or telling them to do anything, or scaring them in any way; he does not seem to believe in it. My mother loves babies – some women don't but she does – even when they are very new; all raw and whimpering and scarcely yet human. Her love is more passionate than his; I think, she can be almost hurt by it. At any rate I know that this is where my current happiness comes from, that the better part of my mothering is compounded of my mother's passion and of my father's benign attention.

★

A woman asks me, 'Are you going to have a typical mother–daughter relationship?' You can tell that she thinks this would be a nice comeuppance. The world loves to remind parents that soon it will all go awry.

I think about this when the baby is eighteen months and every hug contains the idea of squirming away. She will stay on my lap if I sing to her, and she will stroke my face, but if all this loving becomes too damn lovely, she will push or pinch or kick her way out of it, and I think, with some trepidation, of the day she turns fourteen.

She also has a neat line in accident-on-purpose elbow jabs, and great aim.

What about sons. Are they the same?

Fair

It comes on you in a rush with the first baby – the unfairness of it. You become blind with a fury that is not quite your own – thousands of years of rage have been waiting until just this moment to say Hello. Why should your time, as a woman, be so little valued? Why should you be the one to give, and to bend? There will be one argument or a hundred around this time that are white hot. You may reach an accommodation about Tuesday, or even about the whole week until 4.00 on Saturday afternoon. The month of April may be one of relative equity, but that still leaves everything to be played for in May.

You are furious because you know that the weight of it is against you; you have to fight for every half-hour that a man will just assume. Who are you fighting? First of all yourself, and after that the wide world, that considers your time to be of no importance. The actual man may be on your side in all this, or he may not – either way he will absorb a considerable amount of the blame.

By the time the second baby comes around it doesn't matter – you will both be working at this all day and all night: lifting holding comforting cleaning minding chatting playing, lurching into sleep in the middle of it all. Sometimes, even the most enthusiastic father pulls away when there are two: it is just too much and he is just too lonely, or he never asked for all this and who is going to put bread on the table, and why should both of you be bonkers, and what about sex, remember that? This, if it happens, is a tough moment, but who has the time to haul him back in? Besides, there is no point demanding your life back from him – you have, by then, no life left to regain.

Women come back from childbearing like Arctic explorers. You see them in the foyer of the theatre, perhaps: they have lost weight, or dyed their hair. Their faces glow. They expect people to notice them and the amazing fact that they have come through.

Men, on the other hand, try to hold on to the thread of their lives more often, and fumble it through a maze of sleepless nights, thwarted socialising, and oddly soured ambition. They end up tired out and happy enough, or they end up exhausted and bitter; while beside them, the wife you haven't seen for seven years waves across the room, 'I'm back!' and you say, 'Christ, she looks better than she ever did.'

This is not a statement about men and women, you understand. It is just a shallow social observation.

Second Pregnancies

No one gives a toss about your second pregnancy. Get on with it.

Siblings

I was the youngest child. I was very much petted and spoilt and, sometimes, experimented upon. One of my older siblings would strangle me to see what colour I would go. 'Oh, you are turning red now. Oh, now you are blue,' he / she* would say. I still wake up choking.

When you bring home a second baby you must listen out for The Funny Remark. This is the thing your first child says, with which you can regale your friends and family. Here are some real-life examples:

'I am just sharpening my pencils to go up to the baby.'

'If I dropped her, would she die?'

'He's not waking up. I think he's dead. How do you spell "dead"?'

Then, after a while, it is fine.

Toys

Tea sets are good. Also blocks. It's up to you, really – what do you want to spend the rest of your life picking up?

---

*Gender indeterminate for reasons, not of transsexuality (there are no transsexuals in my family), but of confidentiality, tact, forgiveness, libel, charity.

Dirt

Dirt is good for children: it builds their immune system. But perhaps there are limits. My child is so healthy; when she gets a runny nose, the rest of the crèche run a temperature of 105. She can empty the place with a sneeze. I bring her in, all mortified because they must know how low our standards are at home. Still, I try to hold my head high, because dirt, in reasonable doses, keeps a child ticking nicely along. I know all this. I know that I know it. And yet, and yet . . .

Why does a smelly dishcloth make you feel insane? I have always wondered about it – the surge you can get around such objects, the feeling that your life is suddenly crawling with contamination, that you are failing in a most fundamental fashion, you are not fit to be part of decent society, and will become, quite rightly, an object of mockery and disgust. A smelly dishcloth is a thing beyond shame: it reeks of poverty, squalor and a loss of boundaries, financial, moral and, in some infantile way, sexual. It infects language, curdling quite ordinary words like 'smear' and 'wet'. The rot on the draining-board is the rot in the body. Death, darling, death: the smell of the dishcloth is the smell of people dying while the rest of the world says that it serves them right for letting their dishcloths get smelly, in a world that is coming down with bleach.

If you think this is mad, consider your Auntie May, or any other woman with a house-cleaning habit – the raw fury as they wipe and disinfect and gouge and squirt. Who is this fury directed against? Invisible enemies – that's who. There is a strong connection between a clean house and a tendency towards paranoia, which is quite annoying for someone like me, who gets the paranoid tendencies without the bonus of a gleaming kitchen sink. If you are a woman and you clean, society thinks that you are fantastically well balanced and sane, even *you* think that you are well balanced and sane, which is sort of unfair for the people who have to live with you and are not allowed to wipe a spill off the floor with the cloth that is used to wipe the counter, even if it is going straight into the washing machine. It is the sudden screaming, I imagine, that gets such families down.

Look at that lovely woman in the school playground with her lovely children, all scrubbed; the girl in florals, the boy with a baseball hat turned cutely back to front. Normal – ostentatiously so, a pillar of propriety, a devoted mother, the very linchpin of society. While chatting about this and that, she says, 'Oh, I wouldn't let them into the garden . . .' and you have a choice of asking why, or backing slowly away. She is, you realise, completely, fragrantly, bonkers. And not only bonkers, but *justified*. She could talk about the state of your living-room for a week.

Theories about domestic labour always talk about the Victorians, the rise of the middle classes and the discovery of bacteria. So we get the religious connection between cleanliness and godliness – and also the sexual, where a laxity with the scrubbing brush meant a pregnant housemaid before you could say the word 'slattern'. But cleanliness is also linked to tribalism, and tribal slanders – as anyone who has seen the Catholics of Northern Ireland outclean the Protestants will know – and through generations of 'dirty Polacks', 'dirty Irish' and 'dirty Jews' America has endlessly renewed itself in carpet freshener and personal hygiene products. This thing goes deep: to talk about dirt or advocate more of it is like advocating poverty; it is to disgust and unsettle people, and break fundamental, sometimes also religious, taboos.

Not that I like dirt. It is always nice to be clean; nice to be nice. Many spiritual disciplines include tidying up as part of religious practice, though this has nothing to do with gender. If only it were fair, I sometimes think, or even calm, then I would never put the Hoover away, I would build a shrine to the Hoover, I would have the Hoover out, all the time.

But it is seldom fair and never calm. I have not a lot of patience for the madness that is cleaning and have spent many years trying to talk myself out of it. I practise cognitive therapy techniques on the mess in the hall – 'That discarded wellington is not accusing you of anything, in any way, Anne.'

But it all made a horrible sense to me when I had babies. They are so small, you see. It seems impossible that you might keep them alive, and so we labour hugely to keep them free from harm. We boil, sterilise, boil again, we wash, we sweep things out of their way, and when they start to crawl, we tidy the floor endlessly. There is also the fact that babies wear nappies and so four or more times a day we are up against the real enemy in all this, the *Ding an sich*, which is to say, shit itself. Baby housework is urgent stuff and unrelenting for the first eighteen months or so. This means that women who have many babies are saving lives with their dustpan and bleach for ten years at a time. No wonder we get into the habit.

Still, some women clean so much, with so many products, that it's not so much housework as solvent abuse. Housework makes women more miserable than anything else: because it never ends, because they do the bulk of it, and also because whatever provokes us to clean and tidy has its roots in rage and disgust. Some women are cheerful around the house, of course, and many men are not just clean but tidy, but the statistics seem to bear out the idea that men do not feel themselves endlessly obliged in the domestic sphere the way that women do, and that women do not enjoy doing the housework, despite the fact that they just keep doing it. We are slaves to our own heads.

If you want equity in the home, or an attempt at equity, these are the rules. I have honed them over years of sitting down at a keyboard for months at a time and then leaping up to shout that we live in a tenement, and why does no one ever clean the skirting boards. These rules do not apply to households which already contain tidy men.

1. Get dirty.

If you insist that a man raise his standards, then it is only fair that you lower yours. They are probably too high anyway. If a dusty window-sill plunges you into depression, you need to consider the depression as much, or more than, the dust. Dirt doesn't kill people. Wash your hands, not the house. Be careful with food. That's it really.

2. Share the territory.

Never ever, *ever*, tell a man to 'get away' from the sink, even if he is doing it all wrong. Never, ever do that. It is his sink too.

3. Demarcate.

There is no point asking a man to clean something when he cannot see that it is dirty. Girls have been trained in the art of housework from the age of two, when they followed their mothers around asking why the chamois makes that funny noise when you clean the windows. Boys, if we are to believe the stereotype, are running around at the same age going, 'Dar dar

dar.' A man may not, for example, realise that a wash-hand basin has an underside. He may not be able to tell which half of a room has been recently vacuumed. If so, there is no point handing over the Dyson.

Play to your individual strengths. If he is interested in food, he might take over the kitchen. If he likes clothes, then he can do the laundry. The point about demarcation is that it requires total separation of tasks, even rooms, and nerves of steel. You must, on no account, wade in. You must let the washing rot in the drum. You must read a newspaper while he runs two plates under the tap before dinner. You must not nag. You must never, ever, ever do it yourself. You must not break the dirty dishes while weeping and ranting about how your life ended up. Keep silent. Smile. Let him sort it out.

I was fortunate enough to develop a very bad dishwashing neurosis, some years ago. Dishes meant everything: the suds, the grease, the plug hole. I had only to look at dishwater to cry into it. It got so I couldn't touch the things. Oh, happy fall.

4. Get lucky.

After a few years of watching men in an office environment, I realised that bastards don't sweat the small stuff. They let other people make the phone calls, they can't figure out the photo-copier and if someone spills a cup of coffee, they just look at it. They wouldn't know where to find a cloth, they are so useless.

Watch this behaviour closely if you think incompetence isn't about power. It is the weak who are busy and efficient. If you think men don't clean because they are more absent-minded, or just not focused enough – then watch a man who you don't love, so you know what to say to the one you do.

Alternatively, you too can become a lucky bastard. I wouldn't know what a tax form looks like, for example. This saves me many tedious hours, year after year. Which leads me to:

5. Get down off your cross.

If he can learn how to get a blackcurrant stain out at 40 degrees then you can learn how to use a drill. My acquaintance is littered with women whose lives would be changed if they could do this one thing. Actually . . . me. My life would be changed if I learnt how to use a drill. I can design the shelf and measure the shelf, I can source the wood and buy the wood, and get the right bracket and mark the wall and finally, after weeks of this, I can wring my hands, and after a few months of hand-wringing, I can shout a bit and, suddenly, a year later, I can stomp off for an unscheduled walk with no keys in my pocket and the children left unfed, and why? Because I am afraid of the drill. I am, more specifically, afraid, while pregnant, that the drill will puncture my stomach and amniotic fluid gush out.

Really, I do not deserve to be happy.

Other Mothers, Other Fathers

Other mothers are always far too worried about their children, and then far too casual in spooky, possibly dangerous ways. Other mothers ignore their children when they pull at them; then smother them with attention just when you get to the point of the conversation. Other mothers give their children outrageous foods – things you wouldn't even be able to find in the supermarket. Other fathers are too indifferent or too loud and they always get a child excited just before bedtime.

Their children, on the other hand, are fantastic. It is a commonplace to say that OPCs are dull compared to your own, but I really like them. I like looking at them and testing their personalities, at an early age. I look forward to seeing them grow up. I love seeing her father's eyes looking out of a little girl's face. There is nothing so interesting, I find, as what comes out of two people, and how it turns out, this time round.

How to Get Trolleyed While Breast-feeding

Go out. Get trolleyed. Sober up. Feed the baby the next day.

Sounds simple, doesn't it? First, though, you must wait until your milk supply is established, until you can say the word 'breast-pump' without wincing (this may never happen), and until your baby has been offered, and has accepted, a bottle. Alternatively, you must wait until you no longer get dizzy spells while sitting quietly in a chair – which is to say, until the baby has started sleeping for six hours or more at night. This may never happen either. The bottom line is, you must wait until you can stand it no longer – the smiles, the wriggles, the squawks, the purdah of poo and baby bliss; you must press the ejector button just before the plane crashes, which, in the case of motherhood, is just before you run screaming down the street in your nightie yelling, 'Taxi!'

Three months is a good rule of thumb. It may take longer, but three months makes a nice number, as you budget your sobriety, to add to pregnancy and make an even year – no harm in that, it is a cheaper way to live. Meanwhile, you must forgo the professional advantages your colleagues enjoy from falling over in front of each other and laughing it off the next day.

You will become an outsider, for a while. Perhaps for ever. Motherhood can interfere with your drinking for up to fifteen years; firstly because you don't want to drop them, and subsequently because you don't want to make them cry. If you live in a binge culture, like journalism, or advertising, or publishing, or Ireland, a foray every six months or so will be needed to reassure the wider world that you have not gone all holy on them. One drink will not do this. To go out properly, you need to lose count.

But (shriek!) will it harm the baby?

The American Academy of Pediatrics chimes with the general feeling that 'a couple of drinks won't hurt', mostly because they want to approve of *something*, and allowing a drink might keep you off the cocaine. Drinking while nursing is traditional; mothers used to take a glass of ale or porter to help their milk supply – and also, perhaps, in the secret hope that it would make the baby sleep. In fact, a small amount of alcohol taken before a feed makes the baby take 20 per cent less milk. It also makes them sleep not well, but badly, in the three and a half hours after a feed; so that's that myth knocked on the head.

I've done my research, as you can see. I take my maternal guilt very seriously. I dissect it. I put it into boxes. I throw it in the bin. Then I come down at three in the morning and find that my old guilt has been spawning, and there is new guilt all over the kichen floor. So I stuff it back in again and say to myself, *Think, you fool! Keep thinking!*

Alcohol. Breast milk. Not a very melodious combination. But the key concept here is timing – drink after feeding, not before. Many mothers will find it hard to believe that alcohol does not accumulate in their milk. In fact, the alcohol content of your milk is the same as the alcohol content in the rest of your body – it is reabsorbed back into the bloodstream as you sober up. Two hours after a glass of wine, you might as well have been drinking water. There is also no truth to the idea that feeding a child after a drink is like feeding them the drink itself.

Before you panic about the post-partum champagne that made the room spin after two sips, it is worth calculating how much alcohol there actually is in your bloodstream at any given time. If you get blind drunk, leer into your baby's cot, extract it while falling backwards on to your bed and pass out with its mouth roughly positioned at your breast, your milk will contain a massive 0.3 per cent alcohol. If you are actually in a coma and the baby is applied to your breast by a third party, then your milk will contain 0.4 per cent alcohol, or thereabouts. At 0.45 per cent you are dead, so attempts at feeding will fail after five minutes or so. But mostly, as a euphoric (0.03 per cent) or even excited (0.1 per cent) drunk, your blood, and therefore milk, contains about one-thousandth the amount of alcohol contained in a dry Martini. In 1982, Woodwards Gripe Water contained as much as straight beer, i.e. 4.69 per cent.

There are good reasons not to feed a baby while drunk, not all of them aesthetic. The children of women who drink daily show no difference in cognitive development at one year, but they do show a small but significant delay in motor development. There is also the question of the smell. There is also the question of whether they will grow to like it.

Every mother is worried about addiction – whether she breast-feeds or not. It is not just a question of alcohol – every parent is worried about sweets, biscuits, crisps, picky eaters, overeaters, their child will be fat, or anorectic, their child does not love them enough at the dinner table to eat the right food.

It starts early – every couple you meet worries about when 'the bottle' should be taken away from a baby, what should be allowed in 'the bottle', whether a baby should have a soother, and for how long. In my experience, it is usually the father who wants to control all that sucking, on the unspoken assumption that a bit of honey on a plastic teat will lead the child straight to rehab – you might as well write the cheque now. Sometimes, but more rarely, it is the woman who throws all the bottles in the bin, and comes in, beaming, with a plastic cup. It seems that sucking and the satisfactions of sucking are seen as dangerous in our society: it also seems that the mother doesn't find them as dangerous as the father does. So, while the parents row, *sotto voce*, the child hangs on to the bottle for dear life – quite literally: a baby's grasp on a bottle is so strong that you might think you could lift them up by it.

Of course, the anxious, puritanical parent is right – or at least correct – if you leave the bottle / dodie / blankie in the child's control, it will not be relinquished without an enormous, grinding fight. But will it make them some sort of suck-slave for the rest of their lives: a gobbler, a muncher, a glugger, a fat boy, a junkie, an alcoholic? Well . . . probably not.

There are only two small studies that I can find about all this, both of which find a strong correlation between being weaned off the breast at two weeks or under and subsequent alcoholism: this by way of testing the Trotter hypothesis – a Victorian naval surgeon's suggestion that there might be a connection between early weaning and later drinking.

Of course, as I regale my pals with this piece of information over a bottle or two of Chenin Blanc (we do our drinking on the phone, these days), the cry is unanimous – what happens if you were never offered the breast at all? Who will speak for the poor bottle-fed? But of course, science never tells you the most important thing.

And so, I take heart. There are thousands of contaminants in human milk, including the residue of every bottle you ever slathered on to you of Ambre Solaire; but it seems that dodgy, fallible, perhaps even 0.03 per cent proof, as it is, human milk is always better than the other stuff. More gratifying though is the idea that, according to the Trotter hypothesis, harm is done to a baby, not by giving pleasure, but by taking pleasure away. This is why mothers jump and startle and dash to their babies. This is why telling a mother not to pick up her crying child is like telling her not to staunch a wound. This is why we must be as nice to children as we possibly can be – which is to say, fantastically nice until the third Tuesday in May, when we have to jump out the window and run off to get trolleyed.

Because the joy of alcohol is that, if your baby sleeps for twelve hours, then you can drink your head off for the first three of them and, when morning comes, you might feel poisoned, but you will not be *poisonous*. You don't have to get rid of the milk you make in the course of the evening, or 'pump and dump' as the women on the Internet so charmingly put it. You don't have to do *anything* except have a good time.

It took me two babies to figure all this out.

Two babies later, I am out buying the *electric* breast-pump (wince), and running the curtains through the sewing machine to throw on a little something to wear. Two babies later, I tiptoe out of the room as the bottle is applied by sentimental husband to tiny maw. I click open the front door and sneak down the garden path, open the gate with a creak, and realise that I have no friends left to get drunk with. No, that was just a joke. I go to a book launch, of course. I have eleventy-one gins. I bray and whoop and regale. I meet people in the loo and talk to them in a silly voice while having a pee, only to find the place empty when I open the cubicle door. Ooops. This isn't drunk, it is demented. I've had a baby! Get me a gin!

I wave across the room, and hulloo and tell everyone they are looking great – though they all look one year older, and for some it is the year that made the difference. I do not look at my own reflection, ever. I scout around, looking for badness, but I find none. All the great drinkers are dry or dead or horribly stained. No one smokes any more; there is no romance in the air. The lighting is bad and the acoustics are worse and the men look dull. I say men, but I mean anyone – it was never just about sex, the great Drinking Project; it was about serendipity and the poetry of 3 a.m., locked into someone, eyeball to eyeball, talking complete bollocks.

Sometime around 10.30 the damaged little fucker who has been tracking you all night comes up with the same sneer as the last time you were out, and you realise, with the predictable, drunken slump, that you have changed while the wide world has remained the same. I've had a baby! I'm not! really! interested! any more!

Drinking is a group thing and you don't have a group, now – you have a family (damn). It is time to wander out and lose your handbag in a taxi. It is time to scrabble in the flower-bed for your dropped keys and open the door – 'It's only me!' It is time to regale your man with who said what to whom, until the baby wakes up, and he shushes you and gets another bottle while you sidle away, lowing and leaking like a cow past milking time – the farmer passed out in the front parlour, a bottle spinning lazily on the floor.

Entertaining

It is the end of the meal. Two sets of parents turn their children quietly upside down, or pull them backwards by the lip of their pants, and discreetly sniff their bums. Then we look to the Camembert.

On Giving Birth to a Genius

The baby lies on her back and kicks. Thump, thump, thump. Her feet drum the floor. I knock out a rhythm on the floorboards and she imitates me, seven in a row. Then I knock out four, and she does four.

I pick her up quickly and do something else, trying to distract her from the fact that she can count already, at the age of eight months. I say nothing. Fortunately, in front of her father, in front of her granny, various relatives and friends, she doesn't bother showing off. In fact she deliberately gets it wrong. So, it is a secret between us, this mathematical streak. We won't tell anyone else. I will take it for my own burden, and in the meantime, keep things light.

Dreams

The baby is supposed to be asleep in her room, but she is sitting halfway down the stairs, bereft.

'My cardigan,' she says.

Well, she doesn't quite say 'cardigan', she says the sound that we both understand, at this stage, to mean 'cardigan'. I put it out on the line to dry yesterday, and we both looked at it for a while. It looked so nice hanging there.

Then she says, 'Caw caw,' which is the sound the crows make down the chimney from time to time.

She has had a dream. She has dreamt about a crow and her cardigan that was hanging on the line.

So I get the cardigan, and show her that it is safe. We walk out under the clothes line and look at the sky for crows.

'It was a dream,' I say. But she seems to know that it was not real. She has figured that much out, already. She is fifteen, maybe sixteen months old.

Speech

No one else can hear the baby speak, but I can. I can hear her say 'up' and 'clap', I hear 'stairs'. I hear 'string'. No one believes my baby says 'string', but I know she does, because she loves the bit of string that is tied to the door of the car, and she says 'shing'. You have to listen hard, I admit that.

For months we have been on call and answer. 'Ah da da dah,' says the child. 'Ah dah dee *doo* dah,' I say back. This conversation is surprisingly complex, and gives me a new respect for birds, whales and chimpanzees. With three or four syllables, in all their variations, we can say, the two of us, all that we need, for now, to say.

Still, I dream of the baby turning around, and opening her mouth to say something wonderful and long and syntactically amazing like, 'Can I go to the shops?' I know it is in there somewhere − before her first word was ever uttered, there were full sentences playing across her face. The trick is getting them out of there – like pulling down the weather.

There is nothing so exciting as speech. A baby looks at your face as you say a word, and whatever passes between you as you hear the word back, is love and love returned. It is the gaze made manifest. Teaching a child to speak is giving them the world. It the better than feeding them, I realise, as I stand beside the kitchen counter, dropping scraps of words to my daughter's up-tilted face. And I think that all words are sublimated nurture, or a request for nurture, or its provision. All words happen in the space between you and your dear old Ma.

I develop a theory that all writers have Major Mothers, Serious Mothers, sometimes Demanding Mothers – the kind of women you always know when they are in the room. I test this theory any time I am at a reading or conference, I float it across the dinner table. The last time I did this, one of the writers did not answer. He had started to cry.

On Being Loved

If you want to look old, hold your baby up to the mirror. Put your cheek beside its cheek. This is what skin is. It is something that gets loose the more you wear it, like a pair of linen trousers that fit fine, but only for the first half-hour.

I have lived without a mirror for years at a time and quite like it, but a baby needs to see its reflection, so I hold the baby in front of the mirror and we admire the baby in the mirror, then I turn to admire the baby in the room. It's you! It's you! We turn and turn about. We lean in to scrabble at the glass. We touch the mirror with our foreheads.

Mistake. It is a serious mistake to get that close.

The baby fills her skin, I do not. My hair, which she loves so much, is greying and unkempt. I am wearing (what else?) a tracksuit. I have, I decide, crossed that line between living and ageing; between being alive and getting old. And still the baby likes nothing more than my tickly hair and is addicted to my tracksuit's various zips. She looks in the mirror and, Mama! Mama! she says.

There is nothing for it. I will have to have more babies. I will have to reproduce and reproduce; have my adored non-existence multiplied over and over, until I am completely crocked, completely happy, and hardly there at all.

It's Not About You, You Know

I'm not saying that I don't know how to boil an egg, but there was one evening when there was nothing much to eat in the house and I thought a boiled egg might be just the thing, except I couldn't remember if you put them in the cold water and heated it all up or waited for it to get hot and dropped them in then. Also the whole salt thing was a bit of an issue. The baby was crawling, I can remember her sitting on the kitchen floor and looking at me in that leaning-forward, hopeful way that they have. She was also crying, of course, because she was hungry. So I picked her up and waited for the egg to boil, and tried to shush her, but a five-minute egg is a very long egg to a hungry baby, so she was quite annoyed by the time I had the damn thing out of the water and hopped from hand to hand and cracked open – which is when I found that the white was still runny. I might have given her this, even, were it not for salmonella, because she really was roaring by now and it is the hardest thing not to be able to feed a baby. 'I know,' I thought, 'I'll put it in the microwave – it can't explode, the shell is already cracked open.' So in it went, for a minute or three, and after I had manhandled it out with an oven glove and a tea towel, I saw that the white had a strange, plastic, but very *cooked*, look to it, though we would have to wait another three minutes before it had stopped microwaving itself inside. Still, we were on the home straight, so I sang a little to keep the baby distracted while I ran the egg under the tap and peeled the shell off the strange, plasticky white at the same time, and 'In a minute, In a minute,' I said, as the yolk sac exploded, upwards, into my face.

The thing is . . . I kept smiling. I might have recoiled a little with the fright, but I didn't even yelp. Not a squeak. Not a hint. At most, there was a small silence.

Christ, what's that about? It's about war-wounded women dragging themselves across the kitchen with bits missing, saying, 'It's all right, darling. Your Mama's here.' And thinking, 'They've bombed the fridge – what will I feed her now?'

It makes me dizzy just to consider it. That egg was really very hot.

It's Not About You, You Know, Part 2

I put down the phone and say to the baby, 'I just won an award for my book. Your Mama just won an award!' So we do a little dance. She seems quite pleased for me.

Sometimes, it is a lonely business. No, always. It is always a lonely business.

The Moment

There will come a moment when you will seriously consider walking away from it all. You may even take the first steps. Away. Away. Away. You hand the keys to their father and walk away from the car. Or some night, at home, you will put on your coat and head for the door. This is when you find how short is the piece of elastic that holds you. Away. Away. Away. becomes Stop. Stop . . . Stop. You open the door and look out into the rain and realise that there is nowhere for you to go; and even if there were, you cannot leave. You might as well try to walk away from your own arm. And your child, who calls to you (you turn and laugh, then, and come back) will never forget your silhouette as you faced the street that led away from them. They will even remember the rain.

Some people do leave. It is important not to forget this. Leaving is possible. There are such things as amputees – they walk around with their sleeves pinned to the fronts of their jackets, they manage fine.

Worry

You must always check a silence, not because the baby might have choked, but because it is in the middle of destroying something, thoroughly and slowly, with great and secret pleasure. It is important to remember this – you run back to the room, not to see if the baby needs resuscitation, but to save your floppy disks. Once you realise where the balance actually lies you can free yourself from the prison of worry. I know this. I am an expert. Some people, as they mount the stairs, might listen for the sound of a toy still in use – to me, this was the sound of the baby randomly kicking buttons in a sudden choking or epileptic fit. I used to read the 'Emergencies' section in the *How to Kill Your Baby* books all the time. The *How To Kill Your Baby* books are so popular that I assume some part of us wants to do just that. If the unconscious works by opposites, then it is a murderous business too, giving birth.

How To Kill Your Baby: A List:

Too much salt, fungally infected honey, a slippy bath surface, suddenly jealous pets, permanently jealous siblings, a stupid or pathological babysitter, the stairs, a house that goes on fire while you are 'outside moving the car', a child-snatcher, a small plastic toy, a playful jiggle that is as bad as a shake, an open cutlery drawer, a necklace, a string, a plastic bag, a piece of burst balloon, an electric cord, a telephone cord, a lollipop, a curtain cord, an inhaled sweet, an accidentally suffocating pillow, a smoky room, the wrong kind of mattress, an open window, a milk allergy, a nut allergy, a bee sting, a virus, a bacterial infection, a badly balanced walker, a bottle of bleach, all kinds of weedkiller, both on the lawn or in the bottle, pesticides, miscellaneous fumes, all carcinogens including apples, a failure to apply sun cream, the lack of a hat, battery-produced eggs, inorganic meat, cars. You might also have Munchausen's syndrome by proxy without knowing it, so it is a good idea to check yourself for this, from time to time.

As far as I can see from the news reports, one of the most dangerous creatures in a child's life is a stepfather, but the books don't seem to mention them. They warn against mothers' endless sloppiness with dangerous domestic objects, but they never mention their taste in men.

When the baby is eight months old, she cries every time I move out of sight. This separation anxiety can get quite wearing – it is so large and so illogical. Besides, I don't need to be reminded that I'm not going anywhere, I am with this baby all the time. But I wonder if part of the problem isn't my own anxiety when I leave the room. Will she still be alive when I get back? I picture the court case.

'And why, pray tell, did you leave the baby?'

'I . . . A call of nature, your honour.'

He pauses. A ripple of sympathy runs through the courtroom.

'Well, I suppose even the best mothers must er um,' though you know he thinks we shouldn't. 'Case dismissed. I suppose.'

Mothers worry. Fathers worry too, of course. But mothers are supposed to worry, and fathers are supposed to reassure. Yes, she is all right on the swing, no, he will not fall into the stream, yes, I will park the buggy in the shade, oh, please get a grip.

Is it really a gender thing? Maybe the people who worry most are the ones who spend the most time with the baby, because babies train us into it – the desperation of holding, walking, singing, distracting. Babies demand your entire self, but it is a funny kind of self. It is a mixture of the 'all' a factory worker gives to the conveyor belt and the 'all' a lover offers to the one he adores. It involves, on both counts, a fair degree of self-abnegation.

This is why people who mind children suffer from despair; it happens all of a sudden – they realise, all of a sudden, that they still exist. It is to keep this crux at bay perhaps – that is why we worry. Because worry is a way of not thinking something through.

I think worry is a neglected emotion – it is something that small-minded people do – but it has its existential side too. Here is the fire that burns, the button that chokes, here is the kettle, the car, the bacterium, the man in a mac. On the other side is something so vulnerable and yet so huge – there is something unknowable about a baby. And between these two uncertainties is the parent; completely responsible, mostly helpless, caught in an ever-shrinking circle of guilt and protectiveness, until a kind of frozen passivity sets in. There is a kind of freedom to it too – the transference of dread from the self to the child is so total: it makes you disappear. Ping! Don't mind me.

The martyred mother is someone uplifted, someone who has given everything. She is the reason we are all here. She is also, and even to herself, a pain in the neck.

I think mothers worry more than fathers because worry keeps them pregnant. To worry is to possess, contain, hold. It is the most tenacious of emotions. A worry – and a worrier – never lets go. 'It never ends,' says my mother, 'it never ends,' meaning the love, but also the fret.

Because worry has no narrative, it does not shift, or change. It has no resolution. That is what it is for – not ending, holding on. And sometimes it is terrible to be the one who is held, and mostly it is just irritating, because the object of anxiety is not, after all, you. We slip like phantoms from our parents' heads, leaving them to clutch some Thing they call by our name, because a mother has no ability to let her child go. And then, much later, in need, or in tragedy, or in the wearing of age, we slip back into her possession, because sometimes you just want your mother to hold you, in her heart if not in her arms, as she is still held by her own mother, even now, from time to time.

Forgetting

The baby is crawling and I have forgotten the girl who could not crawl. She keeps replacing herself.

What It Does

This is what motherhood has done to me. I cannot watch violent films (I used to quite like violent films), I can't even watch ones where the violence is ironical (I used to love irony). I cry at all funerals. I look with yearning at the airport road. I am complacent to the point of neglect about my body. I shop where the fat girls shop (it is a different place). For months I do not shop at all.

I am more vulnerable and more frightened than I can ever remember being. Some day I will have to let my children out on their own – when they are, for example, thirty-five – and someone might be nasty to them, and I won't be there to punch the bastard's lights out.

Meanwhile, I am nice to a whole range of people I wasn't bothered with before – doctors, public health nurses, Montessori teachers and, above all, other mothers, whether or not they are my type. This sometimes annoys me, but then, also, there are so many of them to like.

A gardener reads a street by its magnolia trees, the house hunter reads it by price, I read it from knee height. I see children everywhere, and they are everywhere surrounded by hazards or pleasures that I check for, even though it is none of my business. 'Uh-oh, there's the ice-cream van.' I look at their shoes and at their hair, and whether they have bobbles or clips, and are they smiling or squirming or yelling the place down. Also if they are beautiful. After which, I look up and check their mothers. I measure them against myself for age, sudden fat, and despair. Then I smile at them a little. Then they smile a little back.

The things we know.

You have to talk to a baby, and smile at it, now and then. You just have to. And all this grinning can make you feel alienated from your real self, or it can make you cheerful. Or a bit of both. Personally, I find it a good exercise. I have no problem filling this smiling shell, most of the time, and the cuddles and hugs and tickles and rolling around the place are great until you have to stop to make the dinner. Motherhood is, for me, a simple thing. This is an achieved simplicity, and I am quite proud of it.

These are the things I miss: I miss swimming with Martin, both of us in the sea at the same time, and no one minding a baby on the strand. I miss being able to walk out the door. I hate, hate, hate, the endless packing and unpacking and re-packing. All that clobber.

Motherhood has made me more efficient. I suppose it would have to, really. I used to delay things all the time. There was nothing I enjoyed more than letting it all slide, the house, the job, the potted plant. I was a great believer in staring into space until obliged to leap from the sofa – an hour, a day, a week later. I thought staring into space nourished the soul.

In fact, there is something vicious about procrastination. 'Oh dear, oh dear, oh dear,' you say, like a little bunny rabbit in a pother, 'oh, will I, oh, won't I, oh darn.' But really you are saying, 'Fuck it, fuck them, fuck you all. *Die*, you potted plant. *Let it all come down.*'

I learnt this when the baby started to crawl. I would look at, say, a safety pin on the floor and think, 'Oh, what the hell, I'll pick it up later.' Then, quite keenly, I would see the disaster I was invoking by leaving it on the floor. Then I would duck down and pick it up. At first I found it just tedious, to be so on the ball. After a while, I found a kind of zen to it, and it became almost pleasant.

Think of how far I would have gone, if I'd known all this ten years ago. If I had been a creature of the moment instead of a creature of the sofa. I would have written many books. I might even be rich. I would finish painting the hall.

Oh, Mortality

When I was sixteen I was diagnosed with lymphatic cancer by a woman GP who checked a bizarrely swollen gland in the crook of my leg and took my mother aside for a few quiet words. I don't remember anything about the trip home, or the days that followed it. I had no reason to, because no one told me that anything was wrong.

I do remember a look my father gave me when I was brushing my hair in the hall mirror. He did not realise I could see him in the glass. I also remember my mother bursting into tears when I announced with delight that I had lost loads of weight. But in general, I was in the flush of adolescence and this was a happy, almost electric time. Every lunch-time I ran two miles to a friend's house while she cycled beside me, so that we could sneak a cigarette. Then we ran two miles back again. They were the healthiest cigarettes I ever smoked.

One Tuesday or Wednesday I went into hospital to have a biopsy of a gland in my neck. When I say no one told me anything was wrong, this probably isn't strictly true. I think my mother tried to warn me it could be quite serious, but I told her not to be silly. I found the operation quite exciting. It was done under local anaesthetic in a domestic sort of room. The surgeon made an incision, and then got his fingers around something inside my neck – not 'inside' in the way that your throat is inside your neck, but inside the meat of it. To do this he had to push and prise his way around the surrounding tissue, and this might be simple, but it wasn't easy. I am reminded of it sometimes, when I see someone working with, say, a chicken – how tough the body is, inside. When he had purchase he pulled the thing loose. As he tugged, I could feel a tightening in my armpits and groin, as the network of glands took the strain. Everything is connected. I thought of the different maps inside the body, the living map of the blood system, that I knew about, and this secret map of lymph nodes, whatever they might be. 'Drainage' – that was the extent of my knowledge. The surgeon was tugging at my body's drains. I have an idea that he put his knee up and braced it against the edge of the table. But that can't be true, can it?

When he got the thing far enough out, he snipped on either side of it and lifted it up and over to a kidney bowl. We had been chatting all the way through, so when he was done, I asked could I see it. In the old days, I seem to recall, children got to keep their tonsils in a jar on the hospital locker so I wondered at the surgeon's slight shock as he paused and then said, 'No, I don't think so.'

I was so chipper and brave during the procedure that I fainted clear away when it was done. After that it was back to school work and boyfriends and my daily, casual, four-mile sprint for a fag. A few weeks later, my mother and I went in to see the consultant and he smiled and told us everything was all right. This was no surprise to me, so I was amazed to see my mother running to the pay phone in the hall. She was shaking too much to put the money in. When she finally got it together to dial, she just said to the person who answered, 'It's all right, it's all right,' and put the phone down again. When I pressed her, she said, 'Don't tell your father I told you, don't tell anyone – but the doctor said you were going to die.' Of course the 'Don't tell anyone' is the most bizarre thing about that sentence, as I remember it now, but that is my family, all over.

So the GP's diagnosis was, to say the least, alarmist. I should have gone to the brilliant, grumpy old bastard down the road, but I insisted on seeing a woman. Maybe this was because the grumpy old bastard threw me out of his consulting room once, when I told him I had my period – 'I can't examine you like . . . like . . . like *that.*' (This man was a god in our neighbourhood. Not for me. My mother told me some years ago that he had died, while out walking his dog. I said, 'And how's the dog?')

Doctors. Don't you just love them? I think of this sometimes when people complain about a lack of GPs in their area. It seems abundantly apparent to me that the fewer GPs there are the better and that people should be, at all times, discouraged from going to see them. I think of this woman sometimes, with her matronly air. I recall a tweed hat – but that can't be true. She must have been bareheaded, the woman who told my mother I might have six months to live, or maybe less. The woman who said the school should be informed, so they wouldn't push me too hard for my final exams. The weeks between the diagnosis and the biopsy results must have been quite a holiday for me. All my faults turned to glories. I might have been too smart and headstrong to live with, but I was certainly too young and bright to die.

I never did study for those exams – I became a born-again Christian with my lunch-mate and we cycled to prayer meetings with naggins of whiskey in the baskets of our bikes, also those big carafes of Californian wine with a wide lid you could flip off with your thumb. We were quite fervent, and very wild.

I hadn't been a Catholic for some years, but now that my non-death was over, it made sense to become in some way reborn. There was also something even simpler. It happened, standing beside the plastic hood of a hospital phone booth when I faced my mother and insisted she tell me what was going on.

The corridor was busy, but my memory surrounds us both in a blank whiteness into which the passers-by walked and faded, as she told me the truth. But this whiteness was not the strangest thing; the strangest thing was the thought that happened in my brain, suddenly, without hint or premonition. My mother said, all in one go, 'Don't tell anyone, but the doctor said you were going to die,' and the phrase I heard in the very centre of my head, the phrase that occurred without beat or pause, was, 'Going home.' Or perhaps just the word 'home'. And with this word, or this sense of the word, there came (I am embarrassed to say) a burst or suffusion, an experience of light, that seemed lovely to me.

This is only true. I am only telling the truth here, about the light and the word in the centre of my head (a place you don't normally hear things *with*, if you know what I mean). I suppose it was the shock. But I have no idea why it should have manifested itself in this way and not another. I have only the vaguest idea why 'death' and 'home' should, at sixteen, have been the same thing for me, and both so lovely. Though, as we know, death is enchanting to the young.

In my second year at college, Martin cast me as Constance in a student production of Shakespeare's *King John*. He was very keen on her rhapsody that went, 'Death, death, oh amiable lovely death, / Come let me buss thee, and kiss thee for a wife.'

He kept saying, 'Make it funny. Make it funny.' After that, he gave up. My morbidity always annoyed and unsettled him. He came to ignore it, so that I could not use it against him. He was quite right.

Some years later again I found myself in a room in England going home for real, with a bottle of sleeping pills, some serious alcohol, and various implements of destruction. I might describe all this (the dark grey breeze-block walls, the striped orange curtains, the sagging student bed) but I have always found that talking about suicide is a deeply contradictory thing to do. It is a sort of oxymoron. The only people who can talk about it properly are dead.

I dislike the self-aggrandisement suicide attempts involve, and I hate the double misery when they fail. This may sound harsh, but those who try suicide are not, by definition, gentle on themselves. Or not for a while.

And, of course, you spend a long time wondering why. I fell out of the world, temporarily, on Easter Monday 1986 – so maybe it was just a Catholic hangover, the remnant of spending my early life praying to a dead body on a stick. Maybe I had Seasonal Affective Disorder, maybe it is genetic, maybe it was me being in my twenties, maybe it was Ireland being in the 1980s.

The older I get the more political I am about depression, or less essentialist – it is not because of who you are, but where you are placed. Ireland broke apart in the eighties, and I sometimes think that the crack happened in my own head. The constitutional row about abortion was a moral civil war that was fought out in people's homes – including my own – with unfathomable bitterness. The country was screaming at itself about contraception, abortion, and divorce. It was a hideously misogynistic time. Not the best environment for a young woman establishing a sexual identity, you might say, especially one with adolescent morbidity and tendencies towards ecstatic suffusions of light, one who was over-achieving, but somehow in all the wrong ways, one who was both maverick and clever. I mean, what do we need here, a diagram?

Many of the people I knew at college left the country in the eighties. The newspapers said that people emigrated for jobs, but most of the ones I knew left because they could not breathe any more. They left because the place did not make sense. They ran away. As, finally, did I.

I went in the old style, on the boat to England with a type-writer and a single suitcase. I didn't quite stand in the prow of the boat, but I had, by then, left everything behind. I felt as though my life had been bundled up and hurled towards this moment. I was going to become a writer – because that is what people like me did. And so I sat, in an evil little breeze-block room, from 8 p.m. till 4.00 in the morning, every night for eight months in a row. And I discovered that I couldn't do it. I wasn't any good at it. I could not write. Or at least, that was my excuse at the time.

Anyway, I woke up alive as opposed to dead, the day after Easter Monday, which is a no-name Tuesday, and then I went to sleep again for another fifteen hours. When I woke up for the second time, the world was very tender and I walked into it, pleased to be still here, or pleased enough. And though I told almost no one, I quite enjoyed my suicide. I felt vaguely fulfilled. I felt renewed. And the years that followed were busy and interesting and good enough, except that I always had this, like a sweet in the bottom of an old pocket, a little yearning something – the desire to die.

I find it all a bit disgusting, now. It is easy to write nice sentences about this kind of thing, but depression functions in the place where people hate both themselves and other people. It attracts complication, paranoia, impossibility, slippages, sneering, and pride. These emotions are ragged and infectious; they happen, not only inside you, but between you and everyone else in the room. The depressive think that they are self-contained, but they never stop leaking misery, banality, and hatred – because it is also a dull state as everyone knows, a grey old thing. God, I hated being depressed. You make all the wrong calls. You get a week of feeling artistic for every two years of feeling like shit.

By the time I fell apart in the fullest, social sense, I was working as a television producer, and television producers have nervous breakdowns the way old ladies have potted plants – it is only what the condition requires. But I wasn't going to kill myself because of television, I was going to kill myself because . . . actually, by then, I had lost even that – the sweet in the bottom of my pocket. And though I functioned, just about, I was in a state of such solid anguish, I would have done anything to bring it to an end.

I was saved by a 'good' GP (they must come in both varieties, like fairies) – who was the first to ask the right questions; he went through a list of them, as he had been trained to do, and referred me to a psychiatrist who got me a bed, two days later, in a nice middle-class home for the tearful, where I fell like a stone, and stayed fallen for some months. I was dosed up to the gizzard. Such tranquillity. Life was like a television set in another room. It was just something we have forgotten to turn off for a while – company.

In hospital, colours come in blocks. You turn from the old white of the painted ceiling to the fresh white of the sheets, you let yourself creep out for a while and live among the curtains of flesh pink, and you listen to the crying jags of women who have lovely homes that they can't stay in any more; a good-looking girl in a pair of white silk pyjamas who walks down the corridor, sobbing, while a nurse guides her by fore-arm and wrist, saying, 'It's only chemical. It's only chemical.' All this as you stand there, looking at the twenty-pence piece that you have saved for the phone, and never use.

Even though no one knows what is wrong with you, every-one is too tactful to visit, or too unsure, all except for two gay friends who have seen everything hospitals can do, and know the solace of a good dressing-gown. Even they seem muted by the nothingness of the place, or maybe by the nothingness in my voice after all the pills. In the smoking-room, one of them looks at a crucifix that is tied to a cable running down the wall. He says, 'My goodness. I didn't know He was electrocuted.'

'Who?'

'Christ. I just didn't know they killed Him that way.'

On which joke, and a tape that Martin brings, complete with a Walkman to play it on, I live for some days.

There was another woman in the room with me, whose life was genuinely sad while mine was only askew. She kept her face turned to the wall. When I opened the curtain to go to the toilet, I would see her shoulder poking up under the blan-ket, the swell of her hip and the useless line of her legs.

The nurse came in from time to time and shouted our names at us. Hello, Anne. Hello, Connie.

She should have been 'Miss' something – Patterson, or Hanley or Maguire. She might have been fifty, or sixty. Respectable in the old style, I could tell that she found the loss of privacy an irritation. Her nightie was brushed cotton to the ankle, sprig-printed, with a bib front that was threaded around with blue ribbon and edged in cotton lace. She had mannish, tartan slippers and the dressing-gown was a pink candlewick thing with some of the threads fallen, or picked away.

It was a week, or more, before I looked up from all this to her face.

I wore a white nightshirt striped with blue that was un-accountably torn at the neck. My mother insisted on bringing it home with her, so she could stitch it back together again.

My parents came every other day and Martin came on the days in between. Connie did not have visitors. Of course she was single and her parents were dead. But there should have been a little rally of women, who divided the week between them and came in every other day. But Connie was alone. She was having her little time.

For two weeks, or perhaps three, we were together, which is many hundred hours; awake at odd times, or asleep at odd times. We got up for a cigarette, or to go to the toilet, and had our visitors (insofar as they could be had) and waited. I did not know what I was waiting for, but she was waiting for the drugs to work. Because she was an old lag.

My parents said hello to her when they came in the door and this made me more aware that I never spoke to her, nor she to me. She would turn away then, out of misery, but also out of pity for my daily visit, and what might be said. ('No, they haven't done a Barium meal yet. Actually, I haven't got a peptic ulcer.') I could tell the difference between her listening back and her not-listening back. She was only sometimes aware of the words that were spoken in the room.

Oh, but she jumped. She jumped for the doctor, when he came in with a smile and shouted carefully about her drugs. He talked about different mixtures, and what they could try next, and he mentioned lithium, so I knew that she was quite bad.

I was bad, but I was not as bad as all that. I did not have a doctor who talked to me as though he was presenting *Blue Peter*, for a start. I didn't look at him and whisper, 'Yes, Doctor,' while clutching the covers to my chin like a five-year-old child. My doctor (who was a woman) knew that I was depressed, not deaf. She did not discuss my medication in front of other patients. I spoke to her in full, social sentences, not in this woman's plaintive, tea-and-sandwiches, 'No, Doctor, I think I'm worse today.'

'Hello,' I said to my doctor when she came in, and 'Hello,' she would say to me, and, 'Hello, Connie,' to the woman I had never spoken to, who must be called by her first name.

'Hello, Doctor,' she would say.

Everybody had to be nice to us. As if we cared.

I don't know if she slept or not. She never cried – she seeped a little. I could hear her seeping, from time to time.

One day, a woman came to visit. She brought her children, I heard them outside the door, the jump-up-and-down of them in the dinginess of the ward. Connie was very proud of them, and of her niece, it must be, who brought them to see her. She came back to the room and gave me a snooty look, as though I had underestimated her, very badly.

191

Still, we were both too tired for all that. Something like that could set you back for days.

After some unspecified time, she started getting her rage back. The whole mess inside her head started up again. I could tell, by the way she sighed, or blinked at the ceiling, or turned away. She was a frightened old woman. She was a five-year-old child. I had the world ahead of me and didn't even bother to be polite. I knew all this even though we did not speak. It was the look on her face: her little tea-and-sandwiches face, only now there was spit in the egg mayonnaise.

Sick. Well. It was all a new language for me. How long before you don't have feelings, just symptoms, just a direction, like Connie – 'up' or 'down'.

It's only chemical.

I had to remake myself. I had to unmake myself. I was a bunch of chemicals. I was a dog that had to be walked, or it would bite. I had to be careful with myself, like a trusted cup that you carry to the table as a child and do not spill. I had to think about power – because I was surrounded by the powerless. I was one of them. I had lost, discarded. I could not manage. I would not engage with, in. I could not admire. I did not trust.

I remember the window; the helpless kindness of my father as he sat in front of it, and my mother, hovering. Or Martin, who has a trick of stillness, sitting with me in the smoking-room. I remember, with some reverence, the packet of fruit pastilles he brought me. I knew, as I sat up in bed and ate them, that I would be better. A year for the green, and a year for the black. I counted them out. Maybe two years for the yellow.

One day, Connie sat up and combed her hair.

★

All this happened many years ago. I wonder whether I have passed her in the street. I wonder if she is dead, or if she is better. Probably neither – a little worse, very much the same. From the way she talked to the doctor (Yes, Daddy. No, Daddy) I would guess that whatever did for Connie happened when she was very small. We were opposites, in a way. The place where she was most damaged was the place where I was happiest. It was time I took my good fortune seriously, and went home.

There is a certain ruthlessness about a recovering depressive, and like alcoholics we are never cured. It takes rigour. No sharp knives. No breakages of the skin. No baths after nightfall. No pockets. No rocks. You must learn to accept many things: that mornings are like this. That some days you will not leave the house. That a survey of 86,000 nurses over 20 years showed that those who drank no coffee were twice as likely to kill themselves as those who drank at least two cups per day. So you must drink coffee. You must avoid nurses. You must eat avocadoes. You must experience daylight. Because you have your likes and dislikes like everyone else, except every choice you make leads in a straight line to life, or to death.

For six months, the medication turned all my thoughts into symptoms, and made me question everything about who I was. It dismantled my personality. The chemical happiness that crept up on me was not a joyful one, but it kept me alive, and after a while I came to appreciate the soggy buzz of it. I had a place to stand. When I was able to think again, I would make decisions. I would change the circumstances of my life, and so give life itself a chance to return.

So, after a decent interval, I gave up the job and married the man and wrote some books. They were fragmented books, because this is what I knew best, but also, I fancied, because I lived in an incoherent country. They were slightly surreal, because Ireland was unreal. They dealt with ideas of purity, because the chastity of Irish women was one of the founding myths of the Nation State (well that was my excuse). But they were also full of corpses. Beautiful ones, speaking ones, sexual ones, bitter ones; corpses who did not forgive, or rot. Who was the corpse? It was myself, of course, but also Christ, the dead body on a stick. And it is the past that lies down but will not shut up, the elephant in the national living-room.

There is an Irish attitude to death that is both quiet and honourable. It is to do with the dignity of the individual, and the modesty of their leaving individuality behind. Hospice nurses are like midwives, they understand pain, and work through it towards a conclusion that is much to be desired. Catholics are good at dying, as a rule. Maybe I was just a little quick off the mark.

My friend, who pointed out the electrocuted Christ hanging from the cable on the wall, died, maybe three years afterwards. I was thinking about him the other day as I was going up the stairs. I remembered coming in to the hospital one morning, expecting to find his dead body, only to see him sitting up, with his partner and parents, eating a yoghurt. This happens all the time – ancient little ladies in particular come back for one yoghurt, two yoghurts, another twenty yoghurts for the road – and these are moments of such sweetness and grace: just one minute more of someone you love, that you would think every second of life was just one more second of bliss.

And then they die. Such a cruddy affair. Real death is hard work, and grief is hard work, and you never do get them back.

Real death cured me of the fake deaths that I had undergone, with all their lyrical undertow. I was too angry now, almost irritated by the whole business. It was not an attractive prospect, after all.

Every year, on my friend's anniversary, I think about what has changed since he was alive – and for many years there was nothing to report, no news for the dead. There were material shifts: money or lack of it, a change of address, unlikely juxtapositions of the people he knew (You went on holidays with who?) but for a long time, when I checked the beating of my heart, I found a kind of push in my chest instead. Scar tissue.

I'm still a bit odd. I don't go out a lot. I have an occasional ability to attract people's obsessions or to smell out their damage. So I like a bit of distance. I keep my small paranoias, a little armoury of them – a quiet, but highly resistant, neurosis about opening or posting letters, for example, and a fairly odd approach to the whole issue of getting my hair cut. But maybe that's doing all right, for forty.

And on the plus side – a family, a marriage, this deliberate happiness. I sit in my garden and am profoundly grateful. And I never underestimate how hard people work at being ordinary.

Anyway, I was going up the stairs with the baby in my arms. He weighs a ton. Between one step and the next I forgot what I was going up the stairs for, or remembered that I had forgotten to take something with me, and into this gap slipped the memory of my dead friend, sitting up in bed, eating his yoghurt. It had been some time since I checked in – a while since I wondered what it was like, being alive – and when I did I found that it was easy. Being alive was easy. And more than that – I had got into such a habit of gratitude, and a mother's worry for the future, that I didn't, I found, want to die at all, not for a very long time. I have no idea when the shift happened, but it did. There are no debts, no qualifications, no big thoughts. And more: I want to burst into my life like a bank robber, shouting at my family and at each of my friends, 'Nobody is going anywhere, all right? Nobody goes out that door.'

It has been such a beautiful summer. I write in the mornings while the baby sleeps and, when he wakes up, I feed him and sling him into the car. We go to a local beach in a town that is full of old people. I watch them: a woman in her dressing-gown and slippers walking up to the water's edge – she must be ninety, and with such a fierce look to her, as though she is going into that cold Irish sea if it is the last thing she ever does. Another woman is even older, if that is possible, completely bent, with arms like broomsticks, below which – far below which – the flesh hangs. She stands in the surf with her hands crooked back from her hips, and she pokes her old head towards the horizon.

I change on the pebbled beach, and hurry into the sea, and swim straight out. Then I turn and check the baby, who is watching me from his buggy, perched on the high tide line. I leave him my T-shirt while I am gone, and he waves and chews it; a little ruckus of colour against the stones.

Acknowledgements

Versions of some of these essays have been published before:

'Breeding' was first published with the title 'Aliens' in the *London Review of Books*, 'Dream-Time' in the *Guardian*, 'Birth' in the *Dublin Review*, 'Milk' in the *London Review of Books*, 'Groundhog Day' in the *Dublin Review*, 'Naming' in the *Irish Times*. 'Baby-talk' was broadcast on Radio 4's *Home Truths*.

Grateful acknowledgement is made to Carcanet Press Limited for permission to reprint lines from 'Night Feed' by Eavan Boland © Eavan Boland 1994.

Every effort has been made to trace copyright holders, and the publishers will be happy to correct mistakes or omissions in future editions.